*"Helena provides a wo
lawmakers, and men in p
solution rather than the p
purchase sex. It is a powerf
the sex buyers' industry whi ... at its core
and highlights how for women it is one of the most dangerous 'occupations' in the world. Helena gives voice to women – mothers, wives and grandmothers – most of whom would have started prostitution as children, spent time in the care system, experienced abuse; and most of whom would have been seriously physically and sexually assaulted and mentally harmed. She also gives voice to and calls out men – fathers, husbands, and grandfathers; those from all walks of life who become sex buyers, exploiters and abusers, to be the change. It is a Wilberforce radical, bold call, for the abolition of prostitution, requiring a national campaign tackling media, commercial and vested interests which portray the selling and buying of sex as acceptable."*

– David Burrowes,
Former MP for Enfield Southgate

"A place where the brutal reality of prostitution is laid bare. As a survivor, I'm glad that our stories are being told; the lack of choice, the abuse, the lack of support from police and government.
Every man needs to read this, and to commit to a future without the sale of women and girls."

– Sian,
A British prostitution survivor

“What we tolerate becomes our norm. This thorough, insightful and carefully researched account of the UK sex trade is animated with humanising testimonies of exploited women that Helena has met over the years. Such stories move the issue out of the abstract, stripping away the myths and misconceptions and forcing us to confront the complex, tragic reality of selling sex. Though never shying away from the hard-hitting facts, this book is full of hope in the possibility of change. Highlighting StreetlightUK’s broad, courageous, and compassionate interventions, we are invited to not just imagine but to help build a ‘new normal’ – a better world in which no one is bought and sold for sex.”

– Naomi Miles,
Founder & Chair, Cease UK

"Every good legislator must seek out the voices of those who are quiet, silent or have been silenced. In drawing heavily on the accounts of women involved in prostitution, with whom she and the award-winning StreetlightUK have worked, Helena paints a picture of things too terrible to contemplate – a hidden, widespread abuse in the UK. But also offers reasonable and practical solutions and the prospect of hope for a way out for the victims. I commend it to all legislators."

– Robin Millar MP/AS,
Member of Parliament for Aberconwy

"I'm proud to know Helena and pleased to see she is using her dedication and knowledge to assist women and support them with this new publication. This subject is complex and uncomfortable – too easy to ignore. Helena is laser-focused on confronting the issues and focusing on women's experiences."

– Mims Davies MP,
Member of Parliament for Mid Sussex

"As a grassroots women's group, made up of activists and prostitution survivors, campaigning for the abolition of prostitution, we are keenly aware of the desperate need for frontline services for women exploited in the commercial sex industry. StreetlightUK meets this need and is an invaluable service to the women it works with. Offering ongoing support and exit routes out of prostitution, as well as emotional support and advocacy, StreetlightUK is a critical charity working on the coalface of sexual exploitation and we are so grateful for the work it does."

– Anna Fisher, Nordic Model Now,
Co-Founder and Vice Chair

"An essential book that exposes the reality of prostitution and sex trafficking in the UK. Croft debunks the myth of 'sex work' and makes the case for a coordinated campaign to end the demand for the sex trade and abolish this form of violence against women and girls."

– Fara Hussain,
Director, UK Feminista

NO LITTLE GIRL'S DREAM

Women in prostitution
and the men who
buy them!

PublishU Ltd.

www.PublishU.com

Acknowledgements

First and foremost: Jonathan, my ever-patient husband, who kept me fed and watered. Thank you for letting me download my latest ideas daily and for being such a great listener. Thank you for cooking and keeping the fridge stocked with milk and for the endless cups of tea. For prising me away from my laptop with the promise of a delicious meal, when it was way past dinner time. Thank you for always being there, supporting me and being my biggest fan. I am who I am because of you.

Secondly: My daughters Amie and Mary and son-in-law Ben – you motivate me to be better every day and are my greatest inspiration. You're the best part of me. Thank you, Mary and Ben, for your kind, sweet encouragement at the end of the phone and Amie, for your dry, clear advice, that left me in no doubt as to whether my ideas were credible.

To the other experts in the field, from whom I have drawn inspiration, notably Julie Bindel, Fiona Broadfoot, Anna Fisher and Naomi Miles: Thank you for the incredible work you are doing nationally. To David Burrows, former MP, Mims Davies MP, Robin Millar MP, Farah Hussain, Sian and all those who sent endorsements – thank you. Collectively, your work is inspirational toward ending violence against women and girls and spans decades. Thank you for believing in me and our work at StreetlightUK.

Special thanks go to Jayne Stokes, Maxine Anderson and Claire Morton, who took the time not just to read my draft but to send detailed comments and feedback. This book is far better thanks to you. To my friends who cheered me on: you made the journey easier as I always knew you had my back. Thanks to Ruth Maton, Sarah Reuben and Sue Sanger. On the days it was hard, you were there.

To the team of people at StreetlightUK, my colleagues and friends. Thank you for being so patient in my absence, on yet "another day" of Helena's writing and for the steady stream of messages encouraging me. Thank you to my board, for backing me and being so enthusiastic about the entire process, particularly on days when the demands of the "day job" took over. To my assistant Paula, thank you for your calm, methodical sifting through countless emails and documents and to our lovely interns Mya, Izzy and Nadia – your quiet competence and enthusiasm were a major help with the research and editing.

A big "salute" to Matt Bird and the team at PublishU for the feedback, coaching and general "you can do it" attitude. Thank you for keeping me on track, especially in the early phases of planning and writing. Your experience and enthusiasm made this book become a reality – thank you.

Last but by no means least – to the bravest women I know, who have allowed me to tell their stories. The resilience, resourcefulness and courage you demonstrate, inspire me daily. It's my biggest privilege to know you and this book is yours!

Contents

Introduction

Globally and across the United Kingdom the debate rages on how to tackle violence against women and girls. If we are to support the individual in front of us, we need to see the millions impacted and suffering in the buying and selling of sex globally. Its scale and nature are staggering and billions of pounds are being made by third parties at the expense of women who are often hidden within our communities. Many are falling between the nets of statutory services without access to vital support – often due to wrong perceptions and ingrained beliefs around the myths that surround prostitution and those involved. Issues around consent, rape and language suggest it's the "oldest profession." This hides the true nature of what women are often desperately trying to escape. The realities are stark for the multiplied thousands of women exposed to violence and sexual abuse daily. Their voices are often ignored or drowned out by the tiny minority holding the media microphone, which distorts the true picture for the majority.

In our sexualised society, women's rights and how they are viewed are contentiously debated. Liberals have seized the conversation, where it has become politically incorrect, even an affront to my human rights, to talk about abolition. Unashamedly I am an abolitionist and throughout 'No Little Girl's Dream' I will lay out the facts and evidence as to why I have taken up this position. I have always been a results-driven person and the current global sex trade makes it abundantly clear that some radical changes need to be adopted. We need a different approach if we are to see tangible results to better the lives of women in the UK involved and impacted by prostitution. We need to act and we need to act now!

Prostitution is a dangerous world that is often being glossed over and, in some cases, portrayed and promoted as glamorous and a career option for our daughters. Educators and even law enforcers succumb to the false narrative and language of sexual "entrepreneurs" and empowerment. The experiences of the majority are neatly pushed under the carpet of public discourse, yet there's a growing mountain of evidence – tangible solutions to the issues surrounding prostitution. In Sweden there are decades of data reinforcing its position and criminalising the purchase of sex. Essentially it legally recognises that prostitution is a form of violence against women and they are tackling it accordingly.

The stigma, labels and language used when referring to those involved in prostitution are at the heart of the problem as well as the discourse around whether prostitution should be seen as legitimate "work." If so, then how do we follow that through in employment law, for example? The reality for most is that it is not a choice, but a struggle for survival. The sex trade is most certainly empowering but for who? Certainly not for most women involved. I want to raise the question many don't want to ask: Is it possible to end prostitution in the UK? Emphatically yes! To address the challenges and make that statement a reality, legislators and law enforcers must address the primary root cause which is perpetuating the sex trade: the demand from the men who buy sex. Not only the laws of our land, but also the public narrative around the issue needs to change at a national level. The demand is growing from sex buyers, so the violence and issues surrounding the sex trade are not going away until we do something.

There is a growing number of men and trans-individuals involved in prostitution, due to prostitution growing demographically and among all genders. However, I have no hesitation in stating that prostitution fundamentally impacts women and should be seen in that light. So, I will be referring to those involved in prostitution as women. A key element of 'No Little Girl's Dream' is to ensure that the voices of the experts – the women involved in prostitution – are heard. Each chapter includes at least one case study where their stories can be told. Individual permissions have been given and identities, names, and in some cases, locations for case study details have been changed to protect and anonymise.

There are polarised and often contentious views on the issue of prostitution. My position is that I see prostitution as a form of violence against women at its core. The terms used about those involved in prostitution, such as "prostitute" or "sex worker" will therefore be in inverted commas. This is to avoid legitimising sex as "work" which perpetuates the stigmas and the labels so often placed upon women.

Social responsibility for the environment and other global issues are in the headlines daily and there is a growing awareness and belief, particularly among young people, that our corporate will can really change things for the better. Collectively, we can make monumental changes if there's a will to do so. Those involved in profiting from the sex trade are also organised and have learnt to evade the system. The stretched resources of successive governments through pandemics and cost-of-living crises, have in some sense been a gift to those profiting from the women they groom and control. Purchases from adult online platforms have exploded with the growth of the internet and in the wake of the COVID-19 pandemic. Fuelled by a media backdrop that is ever hungry for a sensational story, the stereotypes of society's views of women in prostitution have been perpetuated.

How law enforcers and decision-makers respond in this pivotal time is key. In each chapter I will delve into these issues more deeply, uncovering the opportunity to bring real change and to overcome the barriers facing those involved in prostitution and those tasked to support them. If collectively we dare to respond, the solutions are clear. The time to act is now!

> ***No little girl dreams of prostitution as a career choice. For most women involved it's not a dream – it's their worst nightmare!***

Chapter 1
The Birth of StreetlightUK

It was the winter of 2010 in Lausanne, Switzerland. My friends were former students whom I mentored at college – now some of my dearest friends. The scenery and mountainous backdrop were stunning, the clean air refreshing and the people generous, expectant and just beautiful spirits inside and out. They were mostly musicians with a love for the creative arts and who found solace and joy in the melody of song.

Listening to them was inspiring but something pulled at my heart as we sat in the basement venue right next door to Lausanne's most notorious streets – the red-light district that no one dared enter. The pull was strong as my heart longed to speak with the beautiful yet desperate women standing on every street corner. "No one goes there," my friend Steph explained. "If we go in, we're on our own. The police won't come into this area if there is trouble." It was a place with no rules, no laws and where anything goes. How appealing that must have been to those exploiting and profiting from the misery of the women seeking only to survive and to carry on their deeds unfettered and unhindered by the law.

The pull I felt, however, was too strong for me to simply sit on the sidelines. For many months, I had been researching in my home county of Sussex, England and asked questions about who was helping the women who lived just beneath the radar in the surrounding communities; those involved in prostitution through circumstances that were no fault of their own. I had to meet them, to experience them in their environment and to see for myself the reality of their lives. Especially at night, when most of us are tucked up fast asleep in warmth and comfort, they would begin their nightly routine. So we set off on our quest to understand and to meet what I soon came to realise was a group of some of the bravest women I would ever encounter and who would irrevocably shape my future for years to come.

Women's Refuge

For several years before visiting Lausanne, I had initiated a small project, visiting a local women's refuge. This refuge was a house with around twenty women and their children, who were traumatised and often further damaged by the bullying and dysfunctional system in that particular refuge. In partnership with the local Marks & Spencer's, we provided a weekly delivery of their perfectly decent food, which had reached its best-before date, to the women. We were a link into the community for this group of women, who were a long way from family or friends, living in secret, for fear of violent partners. We furthermore delivered the food to them, which sometimes included the best-smoked salmon, steaks, birthday cakes and quality goods. For the children, it was like Christmas every week as we arrived. It offered some joy and hope in that they were not forgotten. It opened the way for the small beginnings of trust to begin to be rebuilt.

I witnessed the terrible effects of domestic abuse on their sense of self-worth, confidence, and capacity for trust after hearing their experiences. I was aware that genuine change cannot be achieved unless someone is willing to reach out and offer hope and reassurance. It was important for them to feel heard and seen in some very challenging and even unimaginable areas. I needed to sit with them, listen to them, hear their experiences and allow them to unburden their reasons for mistrust before I could offer them hope. Why would women believe anyone after what they had experienced, often at the hands of men but also sometimes by women? One woman bravely disclosed to me that her abuser was her daughter. She lived in fear of her and the shame was immense – so why should she trust me?

This made me determined to become a place where the most vulnerable women, those who live in some of the hardest and darkest places emotionally and physically, could find a place of safety. I couldn't imagine a harder or darker place as a woman than to feel that my only option was to sell myself to survive. I resolved not to be another broken promise in women's lives, but to find ways to help them in their moment of challenge. Often, I've discovered that that's all women need. They need someone to believe in them and to help them find the courage, which they already have inside, to reclaim their lives; to rediscover their hopes and aspirations for themselves and their families and to rediscover their childhood dreams.

No little girl dreams of prostitution as a career choice. For most women involved it's not a dream – it's their worst nightmare!

Most of us will have heard our children, grandchildren or nieces and nephews, with an aspiration to become a doctor or a nurse, an astronaut, a pilot or – these days – an influencer! However, no little girl or boy when asked what they want to do when they grow up says, "I want to become a 'prostitute!'" and for good reason (unlike those involved in the pro-prostitution lobby, who would have us believe this to be the case). Prostitution is not an aspiration or a career choice for most women who find themselves involved. We will take a closer look at this, as I delve deeper into the reasons in later chapters (see chapter 5).

The streets of Lausanne were dark and cold that night with a slight mist in the air as we entered the red-light zone. Set on an industrial site, several blocks wide, there were no physical signs to say, "don't enter" or "enter at your own peril," but there was a definite atmosphere of fear and secrecy as we walked into the Lausanne street prostitution scene. I was filled with expectation and compassion, which overrode any hesitation or fear I felt as we set off to explore this hidden-in-plain-sight world.

Crossing the boundary line was just one step into another street for us, but its significance was so much more. Once taken, we were committed. We were committed to the scrutiny of those on the streets, the women looking for business, the pimps looking out for any trouble and the punters wanting to avoid the gaze of anyone familiar for fear of recognition. It was quiet and the night was young at around eleven thirty, with just a few women visible on the main street corners. A few cars slowly drove around, viewing the "items" on sale. We proceeded and chatted with a few women, for me mostly through a translator, to gain the most basic information and to offer a greeting and the warmth of a kind smile. It seemed so little, but in some cases as we discovered, it meant so much. Initially, the women were eager to engage with us, thinking we were looking for business. They soon became suspicious, retreating to cold emotionless stares that gave nothing away, once they realised there was no money to be made.

It was not surprising, given the frigid November weather in Lausanne, that they appeared chilly in their fragile and barely dressed attire, which provided minimal protection from the night. We walked the area, going around each block. Some streets were so poorly lit that it was obvious there was no local authority plan there. There was no plan to protect or illuminate anyone using these streets. What struck me most was the silence. Apart from the very faint chatter of women talking with a prospective customer, the soft idling of a car engine or a few women having a cigarette break, they mostly stood alone; separated and in silence. It struck me what an isolating existence it must be. It was an eerie silence as we walked around. I only had a smile and a few empty words to offer. I felt a deep compassion and anger at what I was witnessing. I felt angry that these beautiful, mostly young women in their twenties, felt this was their only option and their only choice to survive. But was this a "choice?" Was it a choice if the only alternative was hunger, eviction, and domestic violence? I felt angry at the men, who were husbands, fathers, businessmen and the pimps exploiting them.

With every step I took, the anger and determination grew. As I locked eyes with woman after woman, it broke my heart. I could only see her disappointment, numbness and fear. She was hidden behind a mask of indifference and calm, which sometimes boiled over into verbal ridicule or abuse. Through those two short hours in the red-light zone of Lausanne, most ignored us, a few chastised us, and a few women thanked us for coming. The last woman we spoke with as we were leaving, began to open her heart, to let us in and pour out her story and her hope to get out of this hellhole she found herself in. What was remarkable, was that it was to the male member of our tiny group that she saw a place to begin to trust and to hope again. Why? Because he was different to the other men she encountered on those streets. He didn't want something from her, to take from her, to abuse or dishonour her. He came offering hope that there are men in whom she could trust; who saw her value and worth, and who could treat her with dignity and respect. Within weeks of our visit, that young man and a group of others locally began to visit the red-light zone weekly. They took essentials of food and items to keep women safe, but most of all, they took hope that there was life beyond the streets of Lausanne.

I returned to the UK knowing I was changed and needed to act. I set about establishing what a few years later in 2012, became the now award-winning charity, StreetlightUK – a specialist support service for women involved in prostitution across London and the Southeast. The words of the great reformer, William Wilberforce rang in my ears, "Having heard all of this, (and in my case having seen), you may choose to look the other way but you can never again say you did not know."

Case Study

Sonia was a beautiful-looking woman in her early thirties. She was a former escort in Sussex left traumatised by her experiences in the adult industry. She suffered a mental breakdown and was diagnosed with depression, anxiety and OCD. She reached out to StreetlightUK for support wanting to regain some control and live a "normal life."

A victim of sexual abuse from an early age, Sonia grew up in a dysfunctional family. She fell pregnant but due to her mental health, gave over parental responsibilities for her son to her parents and moved out of the family home. She was vulnerable, incredibly lonely and had no money. Whilst scrolling on the internet, she came across a website advertising for Escorts. Sonia signed up for the agency, had an interview and that night had her first customer. She said, "The first time was the hardest, I didn't know what to expect or how to feel so I blocked it out with alcohol." She spent a total of three and a half years "working" for the agency until one day she had a nervous breakdown because of the "work" and was admitted to hospital under the Mental Health Act.

Sonia spoke with us quite candidly about her time in the adult industry saying, "I have been getting support from several agencies, but I don't feel I am getting what I need as no one understands the pain and trauma I am left with. I am afraid to go out of the house, I am paranoid if I go into town and I can't be in certain situations, I feel scared all the time." Although Sonia is no longer in the adult industry, she says it could be easy to go back to, especially if she needs money. She explained that by being in the industry, you must take on another personality to desensitise the situation. She still suffers from panic attacks and is in a constant paranoid state in case she bumps into someone she knows. Sonia went on to receive long-term mental health and specialist support from StreetlightUK.

> ***I believe it's essential to expose prostitution for what it is: violence against women. Prostitution is inherently violent.***

Chapter 2
Prostitution: The Facts

Prostitution Globally

Hidden just beneath the surface, in every village, town and city, the underworld of prostitution is operating day in and day out. The global sex trade is alive and kicking. In Julie Bindle's book, 'The Pimping of Prostitution', her introduction is opened by a remark from a powerful speech by Andrea Dworkin: She asked the audience to, "Remember the prostituted, the homeless, the battered, the raped, the tortured, the murdered, the raped-then-murdered, the murdered-then-raped, "I want you to think about those who have been hurt for the fun, the entertainment, the so-called speech of others; those who have hurt for profit, for the financial benefit of pimps and entrepreneurs. I want you to remember the perpetrator and I am going to ask you to remember the victims, not just tonight but tomorrow and the next day. I want you to find a way to include them – the perpetrators and victims – in what you do, how you think, how you act, what you care about, what your life means to you."[1]

To understand the sex trade in our neighbourhoods and communities, we first need to see the big picture, to get a grasp of the scale and impact that prostitution has globally. According to the United Nations global report on trafficking, "Numbers are always difficult to state in an industry that is very hidden and fluid. Based on several reports forty to forty-two million people are involved in prostitution globally, with ninety-six percent estimated to be women."[2] It goes on to say, "Most of the trafficking which occurs in high-income countries involves sexual exploitation of girls and young women." Sixty-seven percent of sexual exploitation victims are women. In one hundred and six countries globally, most victims trafficked for sexual exploitation are adult women, around forty-two percent.[3] In its 2014 report, 'Shifting the Burden', the All-Party Parliamentary Group (APPG) on Prostitution and the Global Sex Trade reported that ninety-five percent of "sex workers" are women.[4] Furthermore, prostitution relates to organised crime and is second only to drugs in its scope according to the Havoscope website, yielding revenue of approximately one hundred and eighty-six billion dollars per year worldwide.

If we are to support the one individual in front of us, we need to see the multiplied millions impacted and suffering in the buying and selling of sex globally. Why should this matter to me? Because as civilised societies in a collective global community, what we tolerate becomes our "norm." Prostitution has become normalised in our sexualised modern lifestyles and even glorified by some as my "empowered right" as a woman; to use sex for financial gain. But is it normal for a woman to sell herself when you cannot separate selling sex from selling the person? Is it normal for a woman to become the product on sale? At what cost does this come: not only to the individual but to communities as a whole? I will discuss this in more detail in a later chapter but suffice to say, to change the status quo, some tough questions need to be asked and answered as we each take social responsibility for the world we live in.

How big is the problem in the UK?

In the UK prostitution is a devolved issue, so Scotland and Northern Ireland Assemblies are free to legislate separately. In England and Wales, the sale and purchase of sexual services are legal, but various related activities are criminal. This includes activities linked to exploitation, such as controlling prostitution or managing a brothel and activities that can present a public nuisance, such as buying or selling sex in public.

Cease UK (the Centre to End All Sexual Exploitation) organised a summit in 2019, at which I was a panel guest. At the event, Sarah Champion MP, Shadow Secretary of State for Women and Equalities (2016–2017), stated that she believed there to be approximately one hundred and five thousand individuals in the UK involved in prostitution. These are predominantly and overwhelmingly women.[5]

My career has involved working in the charity sector for over twenty-five years, supporting women in refuges and separated families and tackling issues such as domestic and sexual violence. I travelled extensively at that time and spoke at women's conferences across the UK and Europe. In 2010 I became acutely aware there was a very hidden problem that wasn't being talked about bubbling under the surface everywhere I went. Women at the end of seminars would come and privately disclose to me their hidden past which involved prostitution. They often came with much shame and fear of exposure, with not even their husbands, families and closest friends being aware. This secret shame tortured them.

Living in the lovely, leafy market town of Horsham in Sussex, I began to wonder if prostitution was happening there. Nothing on the surface would suggest so, however, as I intentionally began to "lift the lid" on prostitution, I quickly discovered that this dark underworld was indeed alive and kicking, right on my doorstep. It was a shocking discovery. It was notable how extraordinarily little research it took to uncover an organised, prevalent and growing sex industry that involved thousands of women. Most of them had no voice and just a glamorised masked and often false identity online that were scrolled through daily by unknown men looking to buy sex. It was a heart-wrenching discovery as scales fell off my eyes at what I now plainly see and for those brave enough to look, for them it may too be an eye-opening revelation.

The Tip of the Iceberg

Having worked in this field for decades, it's become apparent to me that one hundred and five thousand individuals believed to be involved in prostitution is just the tip of the iceberg! How do you count the numbers of those who just don't want to be found or who are hidden through coercion and control and at worst, held captive in modern slavery? It's an impossible task. Those involved in prostitution move around constantly, so its fluid nature adds to the challenge of seeing its true scale. Economic migrants, often controlled by gangs from Romania, Poland and China, move constantly across London and the southeast towns. Women spend anything from three days to three weeks in one place before moving on in their "tour" of the UK. How do you count the women who are working independently from a hotel room or flat they use mid-week, before returning home to normal family life at the weekend?

I met Jane in a hotel room at Gatwick Airport. She lived in Scotland and caught a cheap EasyJet flight on a Monday, where she daily saw a constant stream of incoming businessmen. She would then return home to her family on a Thursday for the weekend. Isolated, alone and out of sight, she reached out for support to break free from this dangerously hidden existence. Her daily reality was one of bizarre and sometimes dangerous sexual demands, infections and violence, that she couldn't expose or talk about with anyone. It was finally taking its toll.

A Dangerous World

Many charities and specialist support organisations like StreetlightUK have worked hard over decades to ensure that the women we support are seen and heard. They often fall between the nets of the statutory services such as social services, the NHS and the criminal justice system. Just last month a woman we support told us, "I have been doing this for over twenty-five years and you are the first person who has ever asked me if I am OK. It really meant a lot to me.[6] Sadly, we are told this too often. Primarily this happens because of the perceptions around prostitution of the issue of "choice" and "consent." Trafficking victims are rightly seen as that – victims. They are those who have been exploited and coerced into something they never agreed to and had no power to prevent. But for women in prostitution, despite their vulnerabilities being so prevalent, they are often not seen in the same light, because she is "choosing this work, is she not?" Thankfully, over recent years, some local authorities – although not all – are including prostitution and those involved, in their violence against women and girls' (VAWG) strategies and forums.

To me, when thinking about the women we support I do not primarily see those involved in the sex industry as "victims" as all too often that term can also become a label that defines them. Consequently, it can become difficult to break free from when a woman seeks to exit prostitution. If others view her in that way, it can easily in turn lead her to feel that way about herself. However, that doesn't mean that many women in prostitution have not become victims. The definition of the term "victim" is "a person harmed, injured, or killed as a result of a crime, accident, or other event or action."

Violent at its Core

There are many crimes committed against women in the sex industry, which often go unreported and unchallenged. To change attitudes and subsequently change laws that will better the lives of those involved in prostitution, I believe it's essential to expose prostitution for what it is: violence against women. Prostitution is inherently violent. Those involved are often controlled by violence and threats of violence. Much of the recent research globally conducted by professionals, exposes that prostitution is a dangerous world for those involved. In the UK, the 2023 National Policing 'Sex Work' Guidance notes that, "the murder of 'sex workers' continues to take place at an alarming rate" and that at the time of writing the guidance, one hundred and fifty-two "sex workers" had been murdered since 1990.[7] This increased to one hundred and eighty women in prostitution murdered in the UK, between 1990 and 2016.[8] The internationally recognised charity CARE described prostitution as one of the most dangerous occupations in the world, with many sex workers experiencing violence from sex buyers. The All Party Parliamentary Group (APPG) report on prostitution referred to "near pandemic levels of violence experienced by women in prostitution."[9]

The UN defines trafficking and prostitution as "forms of violence against women with both being inextricably linked: the demand for solicited sex drives the worldwide crisis of trafficking in women and girls. The demand for sexual services by women and girls makes them a target for traffickers. In countries where prostitution is legalised, demand for legal and illegal prostitution increases and in turn, so does trafficking."[10]

Intrinsically violent at its core, some would even go so far as to say that a woman is effectively raped each time money is handed over and she is bought for sex. The London Mayors Report of 2015, states that the mortality rate of women involved in prostitution is twelve times the national average. The stark reality is that women in the sex trade suffer disproportionate instances of sexual violence, assault, rape and murder in their "job." This must make us sit up and challenge whether this is legitimate work, as the pro-prostitution lobby would have us believe. How do you make something that is intrinsically violent at its core, safe for those involved? Prostitution is one of the most dangerous "occupations" in the world. Sixty-one percent of the women surveyed in the 2012 study, had experienced violence from buyers of sexual services. A 2001 survey with two hundred and forty women in prostitution in Glasgow and Leeds found, "Half of 'prostitutes' working outdoors and over a quarter of those working indoors reported some form of violence by clients in the past six months."[11]

Sex workers also face an increased burden of sexually transmitted infections (STIs) and blood-borne infections. Female sex workers are estimated to be thirty times more likely to have HIV than other women of reproductive ages globally. Normal HIV prevalence among fifteen to forty-nine-year-olds is 0.7%, compared to 2.5% among sex workers.[12]

Physical Impact: Rape, Murder, and the Mortality Rate

The physical impact of prostitution is devastating. More than fifty percent of UK women in prostitution have been raped and/or seriously sexually assaulted. At least seventy-five percent have been physically assaulted[13] and sixty-eight percent of women in prostitution meet the criteria for Post-Traumatic Stress Disorder (PTSD) in the same range as torture victims and combat veterans undergoing treatment.[14]

Alan Caton OBE, former Independent Chair of Islington and Central Bedfordshire Safeguarding Children Boards said, "Women in prostitution are twelve times more likely to be murdered than the national average." Home Office Government reports in 2014 show that the murder rate for women involved in prostitution is eighteen times higher than that of the general population. Prostitution also pushes women into crime. In their evidence to the Home Office Select Committee, The Prison Reform Trust said that women's involvement in prostitution is recognised to be a driver to the offending of many of the women who are sent to prison. Rape, murder, assault, unwanted pregnancies and Sexually transmitted infections (STIs) are commonplace. London studies show that the rates of STIs are from nine to sixty times higher among sex workers than in general populations.[15] British men who pay for sex have also been found to have high numbers of unpaid sexual partners, putting them at heightened risk of both acquiring and passing on sexually transmitted infections.[16]

Prostitution Versus Trafficking

Modern slavery or sex trafficking is rightly seen as exploitation and the best description I have heard to succinctly describe it is contained in the award-winning documentary, 'Nefarious-Merchant of Souls' by Exodus Cry. In their exceptional global perspective, they expose the disturbing trends of modern-day slavery and state that trafficking is, "The exploitation of vulnerability."[17]

With an increased international movement of people, due to war and conflict, such as in Syria and Ukraine, the potential exploitation of vulnerability has been exacerbated. Sadly, this has caused plenty of unscrupulous individuals to readily profit from the hardship and suffering of those fleeing war. I could list case after case of heartbreak over the last decade from the individual women I have met and supported through my work at StreetlightUK.[18] One woman, when asked about the town she was in, replied,

"Are we in the UK?" She did not know the town and even the nation she had been trafficked to: such was the exploitation she had suffered. It was a group of over twenty-one Romanians crammed into a three-bedroomed house that we found sleeping on filthy mattresses on the floor. All were bruised, malnourished, afraid of the "boss" and earning less than ten pounds a week. However, they had responded to a job ad that offered work, with food and accommodation included.

Unlike modern slavery and those trafficked into the sex trade, prostitution is often seen as a choice. Escort agencies and Only Fans platforms play into this narrative when the reality is that they are often a facade for the same exploitative forces that are at work in the world of modern slavery. I will delve deeply into the concept of choice in chapter four; however, I want to state clearly from the outset that I believe prostitution is not a genuine choice. If you feel your only option to provide for your basic life needs is to prostitute yourself, then it's not much of a choice. If the alternative is to go without food or clothing for yourself or your children or to be homeless or lose a relationship, is this a woman genuinely choosing prostitution or simply someone desperate to survive? That is the choice that many women who have turned to prostitution face. For them, it's often a desperate last attempt to simply survive!

Other Countries Approach

The Home Affairs Select Committee of 2016 states that, "Prostitution is a social issue where there is considerable variation in the legislative intent and framework of different countries, even within Europe. Other countries around the world take different views on the acceptability of prostitution and adopt a range of different legislative approaches." Prostitution is illegal in many countries. Most commonly, it is the sale of sexual services which is prohibited, but since 1999, a growing number of countries have also introduced a form of prohibition, commonly known as the sex buyer law or, "Nordic Model" which places the burden of criminality on those buying sex. It also recognises prostitution as a form of violence against women at its core. The law was first introduced in Sweden, notably at a time when there was fifty percent female legislative representation in their parliament. It is not surprising that when women are involved in the legislative decisions for women, better outcomes for women are achieved. This approach was then followed by Norway, Iceland, Canada, South Korea, Ireland, Northern Ireland, France and Israel in adopting the sex buyer law.

Various policy models internationally include regulations to manage issues such as neighbourhood nuisance and to regulate the ownership and management of brothels. They also take into consideration distinct cultures and social factors, other existing legislation and different implementation policies meaning that, in practice, no two countries follow the same approach. Countries such as Germany, parts of the USA, Switzerland, New Zealand and Holland have legalised prostitution in various forms and models.

The different arguments are based on different moral viewpoints on the legitimacy of prostitution. Those in favour of the sex buyer law argue that prostitution is commercial sexual exploitation of women and girls and incompatible, therefore, with gender equality. Those in favour of decriminalisation argue that prostitution between consenting adults is a legitimate occupation which women and men choose to pursue as a way of earning an income.[19] I will explain in subsequent chapters the flaws in the legalisation and decriminalisation arguments, now backed up by decades of evidence in countries such as Sweden, France, Canada and Ireland.

Case Study

Tatiana was in her late twenties, living in a poor village in eastern Europe with her family. Her parents had traditional views, which meant despite her protests, her father arranged a marriage to a man she didn't know. Within a month she was married with two strangers acting as witnesses. She discovered her husband was in debt to some violent men and sixteen days later, was forced to relocate to Spain with her husband and mother-in-law to find work. Her mother-in-law became ill and needed an operation costing more than ten thousand euros (money Tatiana and her husband didn't have). Her husband borrowed more money from the men on the condition that he worked for them with no questions asked.

Within a week, Tatiana's husband informed her that he was going to Holland and she was to stay in Spain. She had no choice; she had no money. So, her husband left. A few days later she was told by the men to whom her husband was in debt, that he had been in an accident and died and that she would need to pay back his debt. She was forced into prostitution in order to pay a debt that was not hers. She was repeatedly raped and followed everywhere, she received no money and was made to have sex from ten in the morning until ten at night – every night. She was not given contraception and after four months she went to the hospital feeling sick, where she found out that she was pregnant. Tatiana escaped the man who was guarding her at the hospital and sought help from StreetlightUK.

If someone goes into a McDonald's and buys a hamburger, they buy it, eat it and leave the shop. With prostitution, they're not buying sex," she said, "They're buying me – I am the hamburger."

Chapter 3
Is Prostitution Really "The Oldest Profession?"

The Oxford Dictionary describes prostitution as the payment of money for sex. In the Sexual Offences Act of 2003, "prostitute" means a person who, on at least one occasion and whether or not compelled to do so, offers or provides sexual services to another person in return for payment or a promise of payment to a person or a third person.[20] Payment for such acts refers to any financial advantage, including the discharge of an obligation to pay, or the provision of goods or services (including sexual services) gratuitously or at a discount.[21] While there is no statutory definition for sexual services, it is deemed to include acts of penetrative intercourse (as set out in section four Sexual Offences Act, 2003) and masturbation. This does not include activities such as stripping, lap dancing etc. If we are going to change the public's perceptions of prostitution and those involved, we need to look at its origin.

Ancient References

Solon – the great Athenian legislator – was the first to legalise prostitution in the year 594 BC. It was firstly to protect marriage and to prevent adultery and secondly to unlimited satisfaction of all extramarital sexual desire. The Bible, which contains some of the most reliable and ancient manuscripts, makes various mentions of prostitutes such as Hosea's wife Gomer and Rahab in the fall of Jericho. I've always loved the story of Rahab, which shows even the Almighty doesn't show prejudice and stigma toward women in prostitution. She was one of the most unlikely people to become the means of ending forty years of wandering in the desert for Israel, as well as a means of protection for her entire family. She also went on to become the great-grandmother of King David and was in the lineage of Jesus Himself.[22] The history of prostitution goes back three thousand years before Christ; however, even before the Bible there was a woman called "Lilith," mentioned in clay tablets. Lilith emerged for the first time around 3000 BC in the ancient city of Uruk (Iraq). She was a high priestess of the Inanna temple and was sent by a goddess, "to get men from the streets."

It was the Victorian writer, Rudyard Kipling, who first coined the phrase "the world's oldest profession" in his short story, 'On the City Wall' (1898). Before the nineteenth century, "harlotry" was the general term used for paid and unpaid sex outside of marriage. Women were judged by their sexual behaviour and considered honourless for engaging in harlotry. The word "prostitute" only became generally accepted in the Netherlands in the nineteenth century. Prostitutes were brought regularly to the so-called Spin House – a penitentiary for women. The convicted women (criminals, beggars and prostitutes) were punished, sat in a large room and had to spin and sew. Everybody who paid a nickel could watch them as if it were the zoo. The women were forced to knit and sew and were detained for a certain time.

Stigma, Labels and Language

When hearing the word "prostitute," what image is conjured up in your mind? The very word is loaded with centuries of stigma, abuse and in some cases loathing. As one very kind-hearted, yet uninformed local parish councillor in Sussex once remarked to me, "How do we rid the town of 'these' people?" It was well-meaning but completely ignorant of how biassed he was concerning the women involved. StreetlightUK frontline staff have witnessed members of the public, punters and even the police shouting at women on the street from their passing squad car to "go home" even though many of them don't have a home to go to. Meanwhile, our team is confronted with women who are sleeping in a car park stairwell or in a home that has become a crack house taken over by drug dealers. Other comments and frequent questions are, "Why doesn't she just stop?" or "She is choosing to do this." Alarmingly, this is asked by those in our often woke twenty-first century culture of academia, who declare, "It's her right" and she is "empowered" by selling sex.

Tackling the Demand

In 2018 StreetlightUK was asked to take on and develop an existing perpetrator course for men arrested for buying sex on-street to deter them from reoffending. I jumped at the prospect, recognising this was an opportunity to tackle what I believe is the primary root cause of prostitution – the demand to purchase sex by men. With our experience of frontline support of women through our weekly night outreaches, this was a way to not only challenge and educate the men buying sex but to also help shape public attitudes towards women involved in prostitution. It was important for them to look deeper and go beyond the masked and false images presented on a street corner late at night. So, the "You Choose" course was born and has now been successfully delivered to over two hundred and forty men with a ninety-five percent success rate in deterring reoffending across London. We run the course in partnership with the Met Police and local authorities in several London boroughs. One of the questions we ask the men to think about is the labels used for women involved in prostitution. We ask them to list as many words as they can that they know are used, e.g. "whore, hooker, slag, slut, tart, hoe, woman of the night, call girl, escort, brass." None of these words evoke a positive picture of women and are all derogatory labels, often used in jokes or satire. We challenge them on how this bias impacts their view of women in prostitution. But who are the women really behind those labels? They are mothers, daughters, sisters, grandmothers, cousins, friends, wives, girlfriends, work colleagues, and students: they are human beings with hopes and dreams and deserving of being valued and cherished. In chapter five, I will discuss in depth the lives and experiences of the women involved in the sex industry. Ensuring the voices of this hidden and often marginalised group of women are heard, is a primary motivation in my life.

Is Prostitution Legitimate Work?

Over the last twenty-five years, I've sat in a myriad of local authority forums and modern multi-agency risk assessment centre (MARAC) meetings and forums. I've often been told when challenging the term "sex worker" regarding the women we support, that it is their empowered right to choose prostitution as a legitimate career option and who are we to challenge their right to this lifestyle? However, I fundamentally believe that prostitution is not a chosen lifestyle; it's not sex and it's not work! That may be controversial to say, but how can something that is often a fleeting five-minute experience behind a bus shelter, be considered a sexually gratifying experience for those involved? Most men we see regularly at our "You Choose" course, tell us the act of purchasing sex leaves them feeling ashamed, dirty and guilty and they regret the decisions they made that night.

One woman escort described it like this to me, when I asked what she felt about people buying sex. She said, "It's not like ordinary work or an ordinary job. It's not like working in a restaurant serving customers. If someone goes into a McDonald's and buys a hamburger, they buy it, eat it and leave the shop. With prostitution, they're not buying sex," she said, "They're buying me – I am the hamburger."

How can it be legitimate work if the consequences could leave you beaten, raped, violated and with an unwanted pregnancy? Or if it leads you to deal with a sexually transmitted infection that you may suffer from for the rest of your life? At the time of writing, we are currently working with police to support women in London who are being targeted by a man who has HIV. He is intentionally trying to infect women by offering free drugs, if they will agree to have sex with him without a condom. In what other legitimate employment could you expect such consequences or working conditions? If we accept the notion that prostitution is work, are we going to promote it as a career option for our children in schools? Sadly, the answer to that in some education settings is yes! Some of our universities have welcomed to freshers' fairs organisations promoting Escort Agencies and Only Fans sights as alternative career options. If selling sex is legitimate work, how do we monitor working conditions and fair pay? Women on the streets of London are selling themselves, sometimes for as little as five pounds for a "blow job" and men on our perpetrator course have acknowledged to us that they have bartered women down from twenty to ten pounds for sexual services. Men would also often offer to pay more if they can "do it" without a condom. The women we support in prostitution are often willing to accept such outrageous conditions, simply because they are desperate and in survival mode – not on a career-building path within the sex industry.

Choice or Survival Sex

In the latest 2023 'Sex Work' National Police Guidance, they describe survival sex as, "Those who engage in commercial sex because they see no alternative." In the guidance, Dr Natasha Mulvihill (University of Bristol) highlights that the term "survival sex" has received particular attention in the UK context since the austerity measures imposed by successive governments following the 2008 fiscal crisis. This was through a combination of social factors such as the cuts to support services for those in need and cuts to benefits for groups such as those with disabilities, single parents and the unemployed as well as discrimination and bullying in the workplace experienced by women and trans people (some have moved towards selling sex to get by financially).

Use of the term has continued to increase in response to cuts to Universal Credit in 2019 and the advent of the COVID-19 pandemic. For example, in 2019, the House of Commons Work and Pensions Committee conducted an inquiry and report specifically on Universal Credit and "survival sex." The term serves to highlight how long-term poverty, experiences of homelessness, insecure employment, and the cost-of-living crisis can influence an individual's engagement in the sex industry. It draws attention to a lack of resources to meet immediate survival needs; it emphasises the structural constraints within which choices are made and it underscores the vulnerability to exploitation or violence that this can expose the individual to. In short, the definition could be seen as "selling or exchanging sex for food, shelter, drugs, to pay bills or safety.[23]

Additionally, there is a gendered dimension to "survival sex," as highlighted by Mulvihill and by the Work and Pensions Committee 2019 report, which stated it is "overwhelmingly, but not exclusively, women who engage in survival sex."

Signs that may indicate survival sex:

- Bed for the night/insecure housing/hostel/sofa surfing/no fixed abode/'sex for rent,
- Signs of coercion or lack of control of any income,
- Signs of control/abuse from partners/sex buyers/ family (current or previous),
- Food poverty/use of food banks,
- Problematic drug/alcohol use (theirs or their partner's),
- Pay an electric/gas bill,
- The only option in order to survive financially (no right to remain, zero hours contracts, no CV or gaps in CV, maybe a carer).

So, the question to be asked must be this: Is it a choice, if you are prostituting yourself to put a roof over your head, or to put food on the table and shoes on your children's feet? Is it a choice if a woman feels manipulated by a partner or family member to pay off their debts or fund their drug habit? Is it a choice if a woman feels forced through her circumstances to prostitute herself to provide for her basic daily needs? That's not a genuine choice – that's survival. Nothing is empowering about this for women. It is not a genuine choice as most would understand it. To choose something implies that you have options and most women involved in prostitution are involved not because this is something they chose to do. To say they "chose" prostitution is like saying that they looked at their lives and saw a whole list of options or opportunities and decided on prostitution. No, most women get involved in the sex industry because they feel they have no options left. It's a last resort, often a desperate resignation, to engage in acts that they would never willingly choose if their circumstances were different.

The Law

It's true that the sex industry and current legislation around it in England and Wales do empower some people involved but it is not the women. It primarily empowers the sex buyers and those exploiting and profiting from the women engaged in prostitution. Current legislation enables the purchase of sex between two consenting adults if this is behind closed doors and not in a public place. Someone advertising their services online and meeting someone at an address to provide those sexual services is perfectly legal. The act of soliciting to sell sex or soliciting to buy sex (often referred to as kerb-crawling) in a public place, however, is illegal and comes under the legislation of outraging public decency.[24]

I will go into this in more detail in other chapters but it's worth stating that some local authorities in the UK may have a more punitive approach and some a more supportive one. This creates confusion and inconsistency in how the law is being applied in the UK. For example, a survivor in Bristol told me, "The police are fully aware of the brothels that are open and operating but instead of criminalising the owners of the brothels, they offer support to women. The best thing they could do for the women in this situation, is to enforce the law."

Currently, the weight of the law in practice falls heavily on the women more than the men involved. National arrest figures continue to show this trend, with more women than men being arrested annually for crimes of soliciting.[25] Women and men receive different punishments for their involvement in the same crime: soliciting for sex. The men buying sex outnumber the women selling sex, yet women are still disproportionately being arrested. Women are of course the easy targets for police teams, as they remain on the street corners all night long. I believe that we urgently need to see the burden of the law shift away from those selling sex – who are predominantly women – and to see it rest upon the sex buyers who are overwhelmingly men. This can be achieved by the introduction of an enhanced and bespoke UK sex buyer law, making it illegal to purchase sex. The demonstrated success of the 'Nordic' model gives lawmakers over twenty years of data and evidence that such a move improves the lives of the women involved dramatically.

Despite personally witnessing how policing has moved much more towards a victim rather than enforcement focus, there is still a long way to go in ensuring this is consistently applied in practice – particularly in London and major cities across England and Wales. No doubt, under the pressure of local communities impacted by the genuine anti-social behaviours that surround prostitution, StreetlightUK and other organisations' frontline support workers consistently must deal with the fallout of a fresh wave of "sweeping an area clean" by police. Multiple arrests of the easy targets – namely the women on the street – only shift the issue onto a neighbouring borough who are often already struggling to cope. This only provides a short-term solution and merely sticks plaster on the gaping wound that clearly needs addressing. This approach worryingly puts women's lives at risk, as they are driven underground and lose vital access to their networks and support service contacts.

> ***"My options were that I either had to give back all the money (which my pimp wouldn't agree to), give him back fifty percent of the money and use a condom, or 'coercively agree' to no condom."***

Chapter 4
Consent and Empowerment

When looking at the vulnerabilities of those involved in prostitution, we need to consider and discuss the issue of consent. How for instance do we determine consent? Is it enough if a woman simply says she agrees? In my experience, many women involved in prostitution, who are verbally consenting have also been pressured into that position by others who are exploiting them. How is the law tackling this and protecting them? It is almost impossible in many cases to make interventions where that is suspected.

To give an example: Tanya, whom I met at an address in Sussex, is a class A drug addict in her mid-forties, a mother of two children and struggling to fund her and her partner's addictions and to pay off his debts. She pays all the bills, as the flat is in her name and regularly he is physically and emotionally abusive towards her. She is on the surface consenting to her involvement in prostitution, as she struggles to make ends meet and keep her family provided for and intact. She will verbally tell you, "I have to do it; I need to go out tonight." Yet is this consent or consent by proxy?

Can a Prostitute be Raped or Say No?

Developing this issue of consent further, I have been told a woman in prostitution can't be raped because she has consented. So, can a prostitute be raped or say no? The answer is emphatically – yes! When a person says no, it means no. It doesn't matter if s/he is a prostitute or not. Even if s/he agrees to do one sexual act, if someone forces him/her to do a different sexual act against his/her will, that is still rape. Prostituted people are much more likely to be raped than non-prostituted people.[26]

In March, a man was given an extended jail sentence for raping a sex worker after removing his condom during sex. The woman had specifically stated that all her clients must use protection, and he ignored her pleas to stop after removing the condom. The case highlighted the legal concept of "conditional consent." This is the understanding that consent for sex is usually based on conditions. In this case, if such conditions (such as the use of a condom) aren't met, consent is negated. When it comes to sex work, consent is based on conditions such as services offered, protection used and payment. In an industry that is partially criminalised and rife with exploitation, abuse occurs. However, sex workers' trust in the police is low and offences often go unreported. In 2018, the sex worker alert service, National Ugly Mugs (NUM), received eight hundred and twenty reports, detailing one thousand, one hundred and fifty-two crimes against sex workers. This further included a hundred and two reports of rape and attempted rape and sixty-three reports of sexual assault. Only twenty-one percent of victims were willing to formally report to police. England and Wales have seen a significant fall in rape prosecutions. In the twelve months to 2017–18, there was a twenty-three percent drop in the number of rape cases taken on by the Crown Prosecution Service (CPS), despite a sixteen percent increase in reports. The CPS has been threatened with being taken to court by women's organisations, who claim cases are being dropped without good reason. Sex workers are particularly vulnerable.[27]

In recent years through the emphasis on women's rights, equality and movements (such as "Me Too"), the issue of consent has also bubbled to the surface repeatedly. For instance, it has sometimes been overtly talked about in the media that a woman is communicating consent when she chooses to dress in a short skirt or low-cut top. Is that justification for being sexually assaulted or raped or spoken to in a demeaning and derogatory way on a night out? Some would argue it is when it most definitely isn't. In practice just as the law recognises that rape can occur within a marriage, it recognises that a woman in prostitution can be raped. But the attitudes towards women involved when rape has occurred are still a barrier in many instances. This is borne out by the shocking and unacceptably low figures nationally of rapes that are brought successfully to trial and conviction.

If a sex buyer is violent, pushing boundaries of consent and demanding from a woman more than has been agreed, it is exceedingly difficult for women in prostitution to refuse consent, especially for women working on the street, where payment is often made after the sexual act has been performed. Similarly, for women working off-street, the boundaries can still be pushed, even though money is paid upfront. One survivor told me, "Payment was given to me upfront at a booking but the punter was drunk and refused to wear a condom. He became threatening and asked for a refund." She went on to say, "My pimp had to come in and de-escalate the punter's aggression towards me and re-negotiate a price." She said, "My options were that I either had to give back all the money (which my pimp wouldn't agree to), give him back fifty percent of the money and use a condom, or 'coercively agree' to no condom."

Whom Does Prostitution Empower?

Is prostitution empowering? There are indeed a small but vocal group of women engaged in prostitution who declare boldly that it is both liberating and empowering. I've spoken with many and listened to their stories, which are also often full of tragedy and abuse. They argue that it is their right to engage in prostitution, which of course it is and I fully support that right to choose. We are all free to choose whatever we would like to do to make money within the boundaries of the law. However, what I am challenging is that for most women in the sex industry, this narrative of empowerment does not represent them and is not their day-to-day reality. The numerous television documentaries put out in the media over recent years paint a picture of the acceptability and glamour that women are experiencing in the sex industry. It is a very biassed and false picture which simply doesn't exist for the countless thousands of women who get caught up in it and who do not feel empowered. I will speak in more detail about this shortly but we need to consider the power balance that is at work when money is involved. If I am the seller, then am I empowered or am I simply indebted to the buyer once money has changed hands? Having accepted payment for services, what am I going to do if more is demanded of me than was agreed upon in the purchase price? Especially when there is no HR department to protect and defend my rights and the transaction of the services being provided is happening behind closed doors and often kept secret from loved ones? Who is really in control?

The Power Balance When Money is Involved

There is a psychological impact when men pay for sex. Once money has changed hands, men feel they now have the power to ask for or do whatever they like, regardless of what has been agreed. One former escort described the power imbalance in this way to me, "When you are out shopping, you are always looking for a bargain; to get the best price for what you are buying. If you are buying a new pair of trainers, or shoes, you are looking to get them on sale; to get more for your money." She said, "It's the same with men who buy sex. They are always looking for more for their money." She went on to describe how for her, she had certain boundaries – red lines, that she was not willing to cross in what men would ask her to do. She laid that out beforehand with each man, but once the sexual encounter was taking place, the men often pushed over and breached that boundary, wanting to get the most for their money. She expressed to me how at that moment, for her, it was difficult to say no, because she knew that may mean not getting paid. So, her boundaries were regularly breached. Some studies show a lower level of empathy among men has been associated with sexual aggression toward women. This explains why many men simply do not take no for an answer and push the women into doing things they do not want to do, increasing rape cases.[28]

Stereotypes: The Yorkshire Ripper

In Julie Bindels' book 'The Pimping of Prostitution' preface, she gives a more in-depth look at the murders of Peter Sutcliffe, named the "Yorkshire Ripper." She pointed to how the Sutcliffe case brought attitudes about women in general and particularly prostituted women into the open.[29] She showed how the police and media reporting of the murders by Sutcliffe, painted a picture of him as a man who hated prostitutes. However, he, in fact, turned out to be an ordinary, married man living in a suburb in Bradford. Only a minority of his victims were involved in the sex trade, yet in an open letter to Sutcliffe on 30 June 1977, the Yorkshire Evening Post said, "Your motive, it's believed, is a dreadful hate for 'prostitutes' – a hate that drives you to slash and bludgeon your victims." Bindel rightly points out that the mythology that built up around Sutcliffe, meant the police excluded several cases of women found murdered in England because they did not fit the "prostitute" profile. Sutcliffe killed at least thirteen women and left seven others to die. The press coverage of the victims was not consistent and played into the stereotypes and stigmas around prostitution. Victims were divided into respectable and innocent, deserving and undeserving women. This profiling and prejudice meant that they failed to see that all women were potential victims of this serial killer, resulting in slowed investigations around those who didn't fit the profile and left Sutcliffe to carry on his killing.

Is It Possible to End Prostitution in the UK?

I think it's important to understand why people and even societies can normalise certain behaviours. Behaviours can become justified through language, even when the majority may personally feel those behaviours are unethical. The use of language such as, "everyone's doing it" or "everyone thinks it's OK." The implication is that if something is normalised then it must be OK. I began to think about this normalisation of prostitution and how society views the issue. Is it normal or just something we tolerate? To say we can bring a radical change, seems impossible. I believe prostitution is not a normal behaviour for women, just as I believe homelessness is something we tolerate in our towns and cities; justifying we will never end homelessness. Interestingly during the COVID-19 pandemic, within weeks of the outbreak, every homeless person was housed in hotels, travel lodges, premier inns and empty holiday camps. Overnight, homeless people were housed. Why? Because there was a corporate will to make it happen as the right thing to do in the deadly circumstances of a global pandemic.

Can we end prostitution in our communities? Emphatically my answer is yes! When I first challenged myself with this question, it seemed an impossible outcome. With the backdrop of stigma, public attitudes and arguments of the woke empowered advocates of sex as work, could I believe that I could see such systemic change in the UK? I've always been an optimist, a glass-half-full kind of person, but this seemed huge. Yet deep down, I believed and still believe that prostitution should not be something we tolerate in society as normal.

Abolition of Slavery

In the late 1800s during the life of William Wilberforce, selling slaves was considered normal. To outlaw slavery in that context was the equivalent today of banning oil. Wilberforce was a remarkable man, giving his entire life to a cause he believed wholeheartedly in. He said, "God has set before me two great objects: the suppression of the slave trade and the reformation of society." At that time, global business, industry, commerce and trade relied upon slavery. It was normal practice and an accepted means of societal structure across the world. However, no matter how endemically accepted a practice is, does that mean it should be something we accept as OK or normal? Especially if it is profoundly harmful? Wilberforce and his companions knew this and set about gaining the evidence that overwhelmingly pointed to slavery's moral injustice and he did not rest until it was exposed and outlawed. For me, prostitution has become a globally accepted norm, which is inherently harmful to those involved and must be challenged and changed.

Bringing systemic change at a national level is not something we should shy away from, just because of its enormity or impossible challenges. Radical change is something I have witnessed in my lifetime, such as the introduction of the mandatory wearing of seatbelts in January 1983 and the banning of smoking in pubs and restaurants in July 2007.

A Pint in One Hand, a Cigarette in the Other

As a teenager growing up in the early eighties, smoking was normal. In every restaurant, at every community event and in public places across the country, smoking was part of the normal social activity. In 2006, twenty-two percent of the adult population of the UK took part in it. No more so was this seen than in pubs, bars and clubs across the county. From the age of nine or ten years old my nana, a hardworking ex-post-woman from Yorkshire, used to give my brothers and me her cigarette to light up for her. At the time it seemed a very grown-up thing to do with her petrol flip lighter, as we took a quick few puffs before handing the lit cigarette over to Nana. Then when I was twelve, my parents moved us to a small local pub on the Island of Portland in Dorset. As I hit my teenage years, sneaking a crafty cigarette in the beer shed, or on the ledge outside my bedroom window whilst my parents weren't looking, was a regular adventure. Everyone around me smoked – it was normal.

If you had told us back then in the pub that one day in the UK smoking would be outlawed in bars, restaurants and most public places, we would have laughed out loud. That would have seemed ludicrous and impossible to achieve. Seeing such a cultural shift in attitudes and behaviours would have been laughed at, because it seemed unimaginable. A pint in one hand and a cigarette in the other were the cultural norm. Yet on 1 July 2007, it became illegal to smoke in any pub, restaurant, nightclub and most workplaces and work vehicles, anywhere in the UK. The smoking ban had already been introduced in Scotland (in March 2006) and in Wales and Northern Ireland (April 2007). How did this happen and how did such a turnaround and cultural shift take place? It changed the public's attitude to the point where in 2024, smoking is seen as an anti-social behaviour.

"Directly after the legislation, more people were trying to quit smoking and more people succeeded because it's much easier to avoid those situations," said Hazel Cheeseman, Director of Policy at ASH (Action on Smoking and Health). Research in the British Medical Journal estimated there were one thousand two hundred fewer hospital admissions for heart attacks in the year following the ban with improved air quality due to fewer smokers.[30]

In UK bars before the ban, air pollution from cigarette smoke was much higher than the "unhealthy" threshold for outdoor air quality (set by the US Environmental Protection Agency), a University of Bath study found.[31] Levels in Scottish and Welsh bars were often twice as high as in English bars. After the ban, air pollution in UK bars was reduced by as much as ninety-three percent. "There was concern that if people can't go to the pub and smoke, they might stay home and smoke around their children, but the opposite has been true," says Hazel. "We've seen a great shift to people smoking outside, so most children in the UK now live in smoke-free homes."

The ban was the result of a long and national campaign, beginning with studies in the 1950s, demonstrating the link between smoking and lung cancer. They demonstrated the harm and did this on a national scale. Having experienced this huge national movement with the smoking ban in 2007, I am convinced that a similar shift towards prostitution can occur in the UK.

"I went into prostitution thinking it was a good choice when in reality, I had very few options to choose from and came out a year later traumatised and more broken than ever.

Chapter 5
The Women Involved: Who and Why?

Who Are the Women Involved in Prostitution?

I met Samantha many years ago at a women's drop-in that had been set up specifically as a peer mentoring space for women who had exited prostitution in Kent. Sam, as she liked to be called, was in her early forties and my first impression of her was of how articulate, well-spoken and kind she was. I was a little apprehensive but excited to hear from the women, having never been to a group before. My colleague and I had driven around various housing estates before the meeting, picking up some of the women to take to the group. The conversations in the car quickly opened my eyes and set the scene as to what was to come in the group.

Sam sat in the front passenger seat of a small car with my colleague driving. I was squashed in the middle of the back seat between two other women we picked up en route. One of the women next to me started to talk about her cat, with various woes and joys, which we all laughed at and the conversation was going well. In the middle of the conversation about her cat, however, the woman suddenly and boldly interjected, how yesterday her nine-year-old child had declared she would slit her throat! She graphically demonstrated what her daughter had said she would do and then, without a breath in between, switched back to talking about the cat – everyone laughed. Sam and the others in the car seemed unphased by the mixed conversation. I was left internally reeling. My mind raced with questions and confusion about what had just happened. The group dynamic, as I later discovered, was full of such paradoxes in conversation, which came out of the complex and often traumatic experiences the women shared: sexual abuse, violence, coercive and controlling behaviours from partners. The list went on, alongside stories of comfort, care, hope and ambition. These women were amazing! They were bravely tackling trauma and dared to believe that their past and for some, their present, did not define them.

I couldn't work out why Sam stood out to me. As we arrived at the drop-in, unlike the other women, who were revelling in just being together like long-lost school friends, enjoying a shared bond through their experiences, Sam offered to show me around and get me a coffee. She saw I was out of my depth and not used to such an environment and began looking after me and serving me. She was a giver and I wondered how she came to be where she was in life in this peer group. I discovered later from my colleague that Sam grew up in a loving Christian home. She had a stable, affluent, middle-class upbringing, where her parents took her to church every Sunday and brought her up to be kind and giving. She could have been my daughter. She was very loved and flourished as all children do in a secure environment. She had ambition and dreams and was an A student at school and enjoyed her studies. The future looked bright for Sam until she made one choice which was to determine the next eighteen years of her life.

Aged eighteen, whilst at college, Sam met Chris who went on to be a tattoo artist. He was a charming man who was a few years older than Sam and she "fell in love." Within fifteen months, Sam left home and was being pimped out by Chris in prostitution. It took her another eighteen years to get free from the controlling and manipulative behaviour of that dysfunctional relationship. She left him many times but always went back. The shame and stigma of her lifestyle were too much to overcome. Somehow, eighteen years later she found the courage to break free, but now a completely different person – Sam was physically and mentally broken. I saw how one wrong decision had led to years of abuse for Sam. I learnt that day that this could happen to anyone. It could happen to my daughters, my friends; to any woman who may have had every opportunity in life, yet still fall prey to being groomed into a life of prostitution.

Why Women Get Involved in Prostitution

Like Sam's story, there are multiple and often complex reasons why women find themselves involved in prostitution. Many women have complicated and abusive family backgrounds and have grown up in trauma and dysfunction from early childhood. This often means that their start in life includes numerous vulnerabilities, such as broken trust, neglect, lack of education and opportunity (to name a few). These vulnerabilities are then exacerbated by some common denominators, which often include financial instability, childhood abuse, family breakups, substance abuse and neglect. Circumstances can leave women open to exploitation and abuse or make them feel forced to turn to prostitution to survive.

Sharmaine, a former escort, told me, "I entered prostitution accidentally. I needed money. I thought I was going to be an escort, as in 'escorting' men out for dinner. I was blown away by the fact that a man would pay for my company. The questions at my interview made it clear that the men would be paying for something else. The idea of it didn't seem that alien to me because my life had been a series of sexually abusive situations up until that point and I couldn't see it was ever going to be any different, so I might as well have something in return. To me, sex was never about my desires or needs, it was always about being who the other person wanted me to be. I was like a relational/sexual chameleon and I was a trained performer in this area so this 'job' seemed ideal. I could finally make money out of the only thing I felt I was good at.

"I went into prostitution thinking it was a good choice when in reality, I had very few options to choose from and came out a year later traumatised and more broken than ever. As a child I believed many untrue things about myself, I accepted answers from unreliable sources and drew the conclusion that I wasn't good enough and I had to make people want me and love me. Being first intoxicated by the sense of control and the ability to make money, my senses dulled to anything that would tell me to walk away. Having my practical needs met by my pimp gave me a feeling of being taken care of, not realising his motive was control, not care. I hid what I was doing from most of the people I cared about. I defended my pimp and my lifestyle despite the effects on my health physically and mentally. I denied my increased drug and alcohol use. I denied that I felt any shame or sadness over my choices. I also felt like there was nothing for me outside of prostitution. There were no opportunities for someone like me who had mental health issues, no education and no qualifications. I couldn't seem to hold on to anything good so this was the best I could do in my life. Prostitution's voice sounded remarkably like the voice of my abuser saying, 'No one else will ever want you' and, 'If you leave me, you will have nothing.'"

Who Are the Women Involved?

It's often a surprise to people that many women involved in prostitution are mothers, wives and grandmothers. Some are work colleagues, working in retail and hospitality as a day job and involved in the sex trade at night to make ends meet. This surprise is often fuelled by the myths and stigma around the women involved. It sometimes has an underlying narrative that they are somehow lower and not part of normal society. The women involved are wives, mothers, sisters, daughters, work colleagues, nieces, neighbours and grandmothers. Women who go about normal activities do the school run, serve at the cash till or study for a degree at university. These are women who never dreamed they would find themselves selling sex to survive.

The Care System and Sexual Abuse

The facts of prostitution are stark and alarming. Up to seventy percent of women involved in prostitution have spent time in the care system. Of these, forty-five percent reported sexual abuse and eighty-five percent physical abuse within their families.[32] We cannot ignore these statistics and must ask some fundamental questions about what was going wrong when seventy-five percent of women involved in prostitution started as children. What protection is being offered to young, looked-after girls, who already have fewer opportunities and multiple barriers to overcome as they grow up without a home or family? A sense of belonging is crucial in a child's development, particularly in providing role models that children can emulate and no more so for young women and girls.

Trust and Broken Promises

Sharmaine told me, "Before I began working in prostitution, all my abusers had been similar types of guys. They were not respectable, professional guys like fathers, married men, schoolteachers, people in positions of authority and trust. I had managed to hold onto some respect for men because I thought that there were 'good ones' but I realised that there was no 'type' of man who uses women. They come from all levels of society. After a year of working in prostitution, my respect for men was destroyed and I became hard-hearted towards them. I didn't know how to relate to them in anything other than a sexual way. I didn't trust them; I didn't like them. I would even say that I eventually began to hate them." She went on to tell me, "I have learned that there are good trustworthy men and those men have earned my respect. I have learned to live without shame and to help others to let go of shame too. Without the abuse and violation of the past, I have found the beauty in life again. I have discovered who I am and that it is OK to be me. I am loved, I am valuable, I am worth more than money can buy."

Emotional and Psychological Impact

It's hard to verbalise the impact emotionally and psychologically of prostitution on those involved. Two women stand out in my mind: the first I met in 2017 when I attended an event at London South Bank University. It was here I first heard of Fiona Broadfoot – a prostitution survivor and activist of "Build a Girl Project" and "SPACE International." I have huge respect for Fiona and have met her several times since, sharing platforms at various events in London to expose the true nature of prostitution. Fiona speaks with a fierce passion that is borne out of her own traumatic, firsthand experiences. At the event, Fiona said, "In a moment I lost my identity aged fifteen. I shut down, I was battered into complete control by my pimp, criminalised, blamed, shamed and bathed myself in a bottle of Dettol every night."

Secondly, Sarah, whom I met in 2012, told me she signed up for an escort agency, had an interview and that night had her first customer. She said, "The first time was the hardest. I didn't know what to expect or how to feel so I blocked it out with alcohol." She spent a total of three and a half years "working" for the agency until she had a nervous breakdown because of the work she was doing and was admitted to hospital under the Mental Health Act. Sarah still suffers from panic attacks and is in a constant paranoid state in case she bumps into someone she knows. The group of women involved in supplying these services suffer extraordinarily, they have higher mortality rates, lower or often nil educational opportunities and experience violence, rape and murder, whilst also being criminalised.

Coping Mechanisms

So how do women cope? How do they get through another day, another standing on a street corner late at night and facing seeing up to fifteen men a night with a brief sexual encounter? Most women in prostitution develop a variety of complex coping mechanisms and rituals to minimise their pain and survive. These coping mechanisms, however, often create a cycle of more trauma and suffering. This list is not exhaustive but it includes the following:

- Dissociative disorders, e.g. disconnection and distancing,
- Substance abuse that numbs the emotional impact but leads to long-term addiction and mental illness,
- Anxiety disorders, e.g. fixation, memory loss, panic attacks and flashbacks,
- Depression, like sleeping and eating disorders, self-harm and obsessive-compulsive behaviour.

For many women, these struggles become a lifelong battle long after they have exited prostitution; especially where there has been a high level of control, coercion and abuse.

Women often become controlling and manipulative with others to avoid further abuse. This has a detrimental effect on them forming new relationships and integrating into social activities. It can also have an impact on women getting the long-term specialist support they need in order to fully recover from the trauma they have experienced. As a result, women often find it hard to commit to programmes of support due to a lack of trust and a history of broken promises. This can further make women initially behave in quite controlling ways or become very dependent on one individual within support services. A high degree of patience, skill and understanding of trauma is needed for frontline support staff as women overcome the emotional impact and learn to trust and build healthy boundaries.

Sharmaine told me, "I have been in an abusive relationship. He was like a live volcano that could erupt at any time over anything and I thought it was my fault if he did. I experienced how hard it is to leave an abusive relationship. Firstly, because it took time for me to initially realise that it was abusive. Secondly, because I had come to believe that I was the one who was 'not right in the head.' Leaving him would leave me with nothing and no one. 'After all,' he told me, 'who else would have a fruitcake like you?'"

The Impact of Substance Abuse

One of the most devastating coping mechanisms for women in prostitution is substance abuse. Up to ninety-five percent of women in prostitution are problematic drug users, including around seventy-eight percent heroin users and rising numbers of cocaine addicts.[33] There is much debate around whether most women who enter prostitution are already drug users and seeking to fund their habit or turning to drugs and alcohol as a coping mechanism once involved in the sex trade. From my experience over the past two decades of working with women, I would say it's a chicken and egg cycle, which is hard to quantify; but nonetheless vital to recognise the devastating impact that substance abuse is having on thousands of women in prostitution. Pimps certainly use drugs to control women and there is plenty of evidence from our work at StreetlightUK to substantiate that.

Case Study

One of StreetlightUK's support workers first met Sian at a homeless drop-in in East Sussex. She moved to Sussex from the West Country and had a long history of substance misuse. Her story is tragic and needs telling. Sian was a mum of three children, two in their twenties, who were raised by her ex-husband. She says she got married at eighteen and her husband introduced her to drugs. Her husband would bring men back from the pub and she would have sex with them while he watched. Sian ran away from the marriage leaving her children and subsequently lived on the streets of

Liverpool and sold sex to pay for her drug habit. She had some supervised contact with her younger son who was taken into care when Sian went to prison. Upon discharge from prison, Sian went to a women's rehab for two years, before she started another relationship and relapsed.

Sian's lifestyle was chaotic, found to be intentionally homeless due to antisocial behaviour and non-payment of rent. She wasn't motivated to engage with drug and alcohol services to address her entrenched poly-use and was prostituting herself to buy drugs or have a place to sleep. She often arrived at the drop-in intoxicated as was the case when she was introduced to our support worker. Initially suspicious, Sian listed a string of agencies involved in her life. The next time our outreach worker saw Sian, she was again intoxicated and this time keeping close company with two males, one of which was suspected to be pimping her. A few weeks later, Sian attends drop-in and has blood on her face and clothes and is very distressed. Our support worker accompanies her to A&E at Sian's request where she discloses that she has been raped. Sian allows swabs to be taken for the police but is adamant that she does not want to take the matter further, despite significant bruising. Our support worker sees Sian sporadically at drop-in following this visit. During wintry weather, Sian was accommodated under the SWEP provision, which gives homeless people housing support during the winter. She is angry because she is not allowed visitors to her room and is having to do "sex work" on the street but she continues to smuggle male guests into her room. She is forced back on the streets at the end of the SWEP provision and life continues chaotically. Sian is then arrested for shoplifting and again for anti-social behaviour and will need to attend court accompanied by our support worker. Tragically shortly after this, our support worker is advised that Sian has been found dead in a flat known to be a crack den. It was later confirmed that she died of a drug overdose.

Immigration

For the past twelve years, since our work began, we have seen a clear pattern of women from Eastern Europe, Asia, South America and African countries involved in the sex trade across London and the southeast. Many are economic migrants, seeking to support families back home. We need some context here, before judging or asking questions about why they don't get a job back home. In the UK, the average wage is more than four times higher than in Romania for instance. It's also true that the cost of living in Romania is half what it is in the UK. However, that still makes it an attractive prospect for women to come to work in the UK, especially where women are the sole providers in a family, supporting children and often elderly sick parents, with no means of other support. This has left many women vulnerable to exploitation and control by pimps and traffickers, who offer a respectable job abroad with accommodation provided. Thinking they are going to work in hospitality, cleaning or retail, many unsuspecting women find themselves coerced into standing on a street corner in London.

Case Study

StreetlightUK staff regularly support police teams across London and the southeast where there is suspected trafficking taking place. On one occasion we supported Gatwick Police, who were investigating a possible victim located in a hotel. A young Romanian woman, Maria, was identified on "AdultWork" as having several red flags attached to her profile. Accompanied by StreetlightUK, two police officers knocked on the door a few times before there was any response. A Romanian man answered the door and was asked to step outside the room. The other officer entered the room and found Maria in a vest and shorts which she had just pulled on. Sexual activity had been interrupted. Both the police and StreetlightUK were concerned for Maria's welfare and needed to know what her relationship was with the man who had just left the room. He had a lot of cash on him and was refusing to answer questions about where he had obtained the money. He was also refusing access to his phone, so he was arrested.

Maria said she had been in the UK for two weeks. She had no money and no return ticket and had been staying in various hotels since arriving. Maria became upset when the man was arrested and couldn't understand what was happening. Through a translator, our experienced team were quickly able to reassure her and explain the profile which had been created on "AdultWork" and the explicit pictures taken of her.

Maria was not aware of this and was horrified that there were pictures of her on the internet and demanded to see them. She had no memory of pictures being taken but was able to confirm the tattoos described in the pictures were hers. Maria initially denied that the man was her boyfriend and said he got the money through a car business. However, she later admitted that he was her boyfriend. Maria said she was not being exploited, she did not feel fearful of anyone and was simply in the UK for a holiday. However, her belongings told a different story, as they included sexual clothing, shoes and makeup, a giant dildo, an empty large pot of lube, a new full one and condoms. It took StreetlightUK staff several hours talking to Maria to build up trust and Maria agreed to go with StreetlightUK to the police station, so she could view the online profile images. Once Maria saw the images, she became distressed and said she had no memory of when or by whom they were taken. The phone number on her profile was linked to Romania. She was asked if the man in her room could have taken the photos. She said he would never do anything like that and is a good guy.

Gatwick Police subsequently linked the man to money laundering and trafficking. The phone number attached to Maria's AdultWork profile has been further linked to twelve other Romanian girls being advertised on the site, one of whom is six months pregnant. The phone number is being controlled from Romania. StreetlightUK team continued to offer Maria ongoing support. A senior officer at Gatwick Police told us that sadly, the trafficking of Romanian girls is a growing problem. Border Force Officers in the past have concentrated on these flights coming into Gatwick Airport and successfully intercepted instances of trafficking. In 2019, Border Force was not allowed to focus on Romanian flights due to complaints from the Romanian Government stating that their flights were being unfairly targeted. This has led to a growing sense of impunity from traffickers coming in from Romania.

Why Don't Women Just Stop?

Commonwealth Housing runs the Chrysalis Project, which provides accommodation and support in Lambeth to women who have been exploited in street prostitution. In their report to the Home Office Select Committee in 2015 they stated that one of the main barriers to exiting, is the involvement of women in a lifestyle and network of contacts that can keep them trapped in prostitution. Other problems include a lack of national guidance and strategy for supporting women to exit prostitution; lack of funding and a lack of awareness among mainstream organisations such as the NHS. This means that practitioners are not confident about raising prostitution with women and may not know the steps to take if a woman did wish to exit.[34]

StreetlightUK frontline staff regularly assist police teams in doing welfare checks at properties across the southeast, primarily because they suspect trafficking or some kind of criminal activity. On one occasion in Sussex, our staff arrived at a property with the police and met a Chinese woman called "Olivia" who appeared distressed and tearful. There was also a man at the property, who police were keen to interview to ensure Olivia was not being coerced or controlled. Speaking through a translation app, she explained she had not seen her husband or sons for a few months. She went on to tell StreetlightUK that she had borrowed money for healthcare in China and a few weeks later was forced to repay her debts. Olivia was unsure of her exact location but said she had recently been brought here from a property in London. She insisted she did not know the male in the other room.

Our staff noticed a box of tablets next to Olivia's bed, which she said she had been advised to take daily, to avoid getting STIs. The pills were discovered to be antibiotics from China. Worryingly, Oliva had been told she did not need to use protection whilst taking these tablets. Olivia refused all help as she told us her family would be put in danger. In these circumstances, it can be extremely difficult to support a woman who is clearly distressed and afraid but still refusing support. The man at the property told the police he did not know Olivia, but when asked to leave packed three suitcases before leaving. Later that day, Police went back to the property, for a follow-up check on Olivia and found the man had returned. He was arrested and StreetlightUK continued to reach out to support Olivia.

On a separate operation, we met Grace at an address in Surrey. She explained that none of her friends and family are aware of what she is doing and believe she is a cleaner. Grace fled Africa with her teenage son three years ago to escape her violent husband. She did originally start as a cleaner when she came to the UK but she struggles with her mental health as has no friends or family she can talk with.

It's clear that women like Olivia and Grace need a lot of support to exit prostitution. It can be a complex and sometimes dangerous time for women as they seek support to exit. In their evidence to the Home Office

Select Committee in 2015, The Prison Reform Trust said, "Support to exit prostitution is one of the National Offender Management Service's Nine Pathways to reduce reoffending." It recommended the development of local multi-agency partnerships that enable women to exit prostitution and a coherent funding strategy for women's support services. I wholeheartedly agree! We must invest in joint services that break the cycles of trauma and exploitation that many women find themselves trapped in. I will dig more deeply into this in the last chapter, where I lay out some tangible solutions.

> ***As I asked Ali and the other men on the course that day, "Whom, if anyone, have you told you are here?" Ali said, "I've told my wife!"***

Chapter 6
Sex Buyers: Would You Marry a Prostitute?

Since StreetlightUK began in 2012, I have been very aware that the sex trade is driven by demand. It is a supply and demand industry – the demand from men wanting to purchase sex from women. Most of our work as a charity is rightly focused on supporting women involved in prostitution, their complex needs and the challenges they face; particularly when they try to exit. Much of our work is supporting women who are trying to simply survive through prostitution on a day-to-day basis. With this backdrop, I've always had an underlying desire to address what I consider to be the root cause driving prostitution – the demand! There's a huge disparity between the nine out of ten women selling sex who tell us they don't want to do it, and the one hundred percent of men buying sex who do!

In 2018 I was presented with an opportunity to work with a London borough, which was already delivering a perpetrator course alongside the Met police. The local authority recognised they wanted to involve a specialist women's service; enabling the absolute best understanding to be brought to the men arrested and referred to the course. So, I set about researching and developing what has now become the successful "You Choose" deterring reoffending course. The course is focused on educating perpetrators – men arrested for buying sex on-street. Of the men caught in the act of curb-crawling and soliciting for sex, many are first-time offenders. Some have been engaged in buying sex on-street for years but have never been caught and arrested. The course is now operating in a growing number of boroughs across London, helping to tackle the demand from sex buyers and curb-crawling the streets of London nightly.

Since 2019 we have seen over two hundred and forty men complete the course and overall, we are seeing a ninety-five percent (and in some boroughs a hundred percent success rate), in deterring reoffending. As well as seeing some dramatic changes in men's attitudes towards women in prostitution, our primary goal is to deter men from ever curb-crawling and buying sex again. We aim to bring them to a point of deep understanding of the impact on the women, themselves and society if they continue to do so. Ninety-five percent of the men who attend the course, do come to that conclusion for themselves. Though non-judgmental, the course is very hard-hitting and challenging.

I'm under no illusion and realise that often the reasons men give as to why they won't purchase sex again, are very self-centred. "I don't want to lose my marriage," "I don't want to get an infection," or "I don't want to lose my job," they tell us. Very occasionally we have someone like Jim who is a retired teacher; arrested and referred to our course. From the outset, Jim was very engaged in the course as it progressed and became increasingly emotionally upset. The realisation dawned on him when he saw his involvement as a major contributor to the issue of on-street prostitution. He had a long-term partner and said he felt guilty about betraying her. He became very tearful when talking about his lack of awareness of the lives of women in prostitution. He left the course saying, "I am determined to be part of the solution, rather than the problem."

I believe that most men fundamentally know that buying sex is wrong. The comments from men buying sex who have attended our "You Choose" course, undergird this belief. They regularly tell us, "The choice I made that day was wrong," "Women involved are not doing this by choice," "I will make better decisions and think before I act," "This made me understand the consequences of my actions," "This made me feel responsible about the role that I could play in speaking with other men," "Be respectful to women," "The dangers of prostitution for 'sex workers' and the situation they are in," "Opened my eyes to how this can impact anyone, i.e. my children, mum, sister etc." The men tell us they feel, "dirty, ashamed, disgusted with myself, guilty of hiding it from my partner, scared – mostly of being found out."

Would You Marry a Prostitute?

Sadly, and all too often, we encounter men who are entrenched in a false view of why women are involved in prostitution. Men who have told us, "It is an easy job for her ... easy money," "She has chosen to do this job," and "Whatever you want you can do with that woman." During the "You Choose" course when looking at the stigmas and labels that are associated with women in prostitution, we ask the men a question: Would you marry a woman involved in prostitution? Of the hundreds of men who have attended the course, I could count on one hand the number of men who have said yes. We challenge them to think about how hypocritical many would say that is; bearing in mind that they are in a room, on a course they don't want to be on, having been arrested for buying sex on-street. What makes it acceptable for them to purchase sex, but hypocritically say they would not want to marry someone who was selling sex? Their answers are self-exposing as we dig deeper, asking them to explain their reasons. "I want my woman to be just with me," "She's sleeping with other men," "I might catch something." The penny begins to drop for many at this point, of the dehumanisation of women in the sex industry that is deeply rooted in the thinking of those who buy sex: that somehow women in prostitution are different from "normal" women and it's OK, therefore, to treat them with less worth than they would a wife or partner. Wolpert found that those who buy sex, on average, have less empathy for women in prostitution and view them as intrinsically different from other women. His report also showed that those who use prostitutes share some key characteristics with men at risk of committing sexually violent acts."[35]

Who Are the Sex Buyers?

The demand for commercial sex in the UK has been estimated more thoroughly than ever before in an analysis of more than five thousand British men aged between twenty to seventy-four. It claims twelve percent use prostitutes – well above the one in ten calculated by earlier studies. Dr Locatelli and co-author Dr Steinar Strom said, "The expected number of times with 'prostitutes' was much higher among men travelling abroad, living in London and middle rather than high or low earners."

Dr Locatelli said, "It could be that the lower income men cannot afford to have sex with 'prostitutes' and the rich men may have too much reputation to lose if they are caught being with 'prostitutes.' Worryingly, drug users and men who do not use condoms are also more likely to have sex with 'prostitutes', exposing them and women to health risks. Moreover, we find that drug users and men declaring that they are religious, are more inclined to participate in the sex market."[36]

Having spoken at many hundreds of churches and organisations across the UK, Europe, Africa, Asia and the Middle East, sadly my experience bears out these findings; that it is a much bigger issue within churches, mosques and synagogues than most would like to admit. This is also borne out by those attending the "You Choose" perpetrator course. It is not unusual to have men on the course, who are involved in the charity sector or faith communities, particularly Muslims, in London.

According to 'The Penguin Atlas of Human Sexual Behaviour' by Judith Mackay, in total, the average British person has sex two thousand, five hundred and eighty times during his or her lifetime, with five different people. British citizens are also the most unfaithful in Europe, with forty-two percent admitting to sexual infidelity.

We live in a society in which, among certain groups of men, there is a belief that they have a right to sex in all circumstances, even if a woman is forced. Men's desires are often more important than the physical and emotional well-being and sexual self-determination of women. In

London, one in ten men has paid for sex and eight out of ten men's first-time experience of prostitution is encouraged, or accompanied, by a male friend or family member. This exposes a culture of acceptability among some groups of men in the UK where paying for sex, whether it be at a brothel, escort agency or as part of a stag trip to Amsterdam, is seen as OK. This is having a damaging and devastating effect on young men's relationships and views of women. Is it a surprise when role models – Celebrities, Pop Stars, Actors, top Athletes, or World Leaders – have all been in the news for accusations of paying for sex? British men are known as one of the highest consumers in the sex tourism industry, with individuals and groups of men regularly travelling to Holland, Germany and Asia to buy sex. The purchase of sex is not only seen as OK but something to be celebrated and done as a group.

The underlying mechanisms and reasons for buying sex are complex and diverse. Additionally, studies have described that reasons for buying sex vary across groups of men and also include, for example, emotions, need for intimacy, social connectedness and wanting a relationship.[37] In our increasingly sexualised and individualistic society, it is not surprising that on our perpetrator course, we see plenty of examples of men with sex addictions and relationship dysfunction.

What Women Think

Men have told us that they think the women they pay regularly for sex are their friends as they are always smiling. They fail to see the facade and mask that women must put on as actors to carry out what is asked of them. On the other hand, the women tell us they think men who buy sex are, "dirty old men," "smelly and overweight" and "that I hate men." Some men also seem deluded into thinking that women enjoy prostituting themselves and that it is a pleasurable sexual experience for them. I have to say in my twenty-five years of supporting thousands of women, I have rarely heard a woman say she "enjoys" prostitution. I say this with the backdrop of a one-sided and often distorted view played out in the media by a miniscule percentage of women promoting prostitution.

Women have told us, particularly once they have exited prostitution, "I felt sick to my stomach with shame and disgust" and "I didn't know that I would begin to feel more like a product and less like a person." "There is no way out and no one to ask for help. The gut-wrenching shame of who you've become makes it impossible to even imagine reaching out to anyone." "All that matters is that I did it and I can never undo it. There is no escaping it." These are not the comments you would expect to hear from women enjoying prostitution.

Being involved in dealing with trauma daily can easily warp a person's view. So, it's heartening at times, to hear others echo my thoughts about the treatment of women in prostitution. I'm very aware that many people, including many men, are horrified at how some men view women and sex. I hear others question how a man can pay to have sex in a bed that he knows multiple other men have been in before him; or, how a five-minute encounter with a woman you don't know in a dark corner of a car park, constitutes a sexually satisfying experience. I also hear people ask why men don't question that the women involved might be forced – a fact that we highlight in our perpetrator course. Most men are not aware that the Policing and Crime Act 2009 makes it illegal to pay for sex with a prostitute who has been subjected to force and this is a strict liability offence. Men can go to prison even if they didn't know the woman was forced.

Misogyny and the Gender War

A few years ago, I was invited to go to a business conference in Birmingham. I was there with a colleague who was introducing me to his Business. The conference was hosted in a smart hotel at which all the delegates were staying. There were several hundred of us, mostly men and the keynote speaker was the former Internationally known, England Rugby player and coach, Sir Clive Woodward OBE. It was a superb speech given by Sir Clive, who described in detail how he prepared and trained the England rugby squad, which went on to win the 2003 Rugby World Cup against Australia. In his speech he gave a real insight into teamwork and preparing for the pressure points that will inevitably come. It was a brilliant message about thinking correctly under pressure (TCUP), which I still remember and quote from to this day. However, my memories of that conference are vividly marked by what happened at the evening entertainment arranged by the hosts.

The hosts of the conference brought in an after-dinner comedy act to entertain the delegates. Having enjoyed the great food, we settled in for the entertainment, as the comedian took to the platform. The next thirty minutes, I can only describe as horrendous misogyny and verbal abuse. The content of his material was not only very below the belt, but every joke was overtly ripping women apart: how they looked, their character, their competence. I was in shock and became extremely angry. As I looked around the room, which was full of teams of mostly men, many of them in their twenties and thirties, I was angry at what was being sown into their thinking. Looking at the few other women present, some joined in the laughing nervously, whilst others like myself just looked extremely uncomfortable and unimpressed. A young woman opposite me seemed increasingly distressed as the jokes went on. There was an acceptability in the room that it's OK to have "fun" at the expense of women and other cultures.

Among my friends, I am known to enjoy a joke about the fact that men are from Mars and women are from Venus. There is of course an appropriate way to have fun at each other's expense, in a light-hearted way. I grew up with three brothers, so I learnt early in life that most men mildly "insult" one another regularly, as a form of endearment. It's how men are in their banter and communication, particularly when in groups. But this was crossing a line – an excessively big red one. The jokes were below the belt and demeaning of women in a way I had never witnessed before. Women, Jews and foreigners were all up for grabs in the insults and insinuations pouring out of the comedian. Several women and a few younger men left and I could take no more, after thirty minutes. As I travelled in the lift to my room, I met the young woman who had sat opposite me, now in floods of tears. It transpired she was BME, Jewish and a woman, so everything about her had been ripped apart publicly that night. I wrote to the hosts after the event and left them in no uncertainty about the impact of their choice of entertainment. I also challenged how they expected more women to be involved in business with this as a backdrop, let alone their influence on the young men present. The sad reality is that I knew most of those who attended the event, simply laughed off and dismissed any uncomfortable feelings in what was being portrayed about women.

Women in the Media

What has this got to do with prostitution? In my view it has everything to do with it, as it is just one example of many I could personally give as a woman: the way society and particularly men see and speak about women. This narrative is played out in business forums across the UK and the Media generally. Women are still sexualised, as evidenced in many high street shop front displays, or television adverts, in which women are either scantily clad or draped over an object being promoted. When it comes to the Media's coverage of prostitution, it is broadly biassed. Over the years I have met some fantastic people in the press, who want to make a difference and use their platforms positively. However, the woke agenda that promotes a woman's right to sell sex and be empowered is dominating the public's perspective regarding selling sex.

I receive press requests weekly. Nine times out of ten, they simply want access to the women we support, which often causes women to be re-traumatised if allowed. Why? Since sensationalism is what generates revenue, the majority of media and press organisations are driven by the desire for a story. The media frequently fails to comprehend that just because a woman is anonymous, it doesn't mean that she isn't being used and exploited again. And the women know this! I learnt early on in my work with StreetlightUK, that protecting women from the media and press was going to be an ongoing battle.

The Impact on Families

Prostitution can rip families apart. Most of the men that attend our deterring reoffending course have come on the course in secret. That is, most of them have not told anyone that they have been arrested and received a caution or that they are attending a perpetrator course. The reasons for that are fairly obvious. We always ask the men if they have told anyone they are on the course as it is a good indicator of several things (such as remorse and taking responsibility for their actions). Occasionally one of the men may have told a friend or a work colleague, but only once has anyone ever told me that he told his wife. Ali was married with young children and from the moment he walked into the classroom where the course was being delivered, he looked broken. He arrived early and spoke softly and politely as he took his seat. He quietly filled in the paperwork for registration and sat attentively, as the other men took their places alongside him. I started to deliver the course and observed he was quiet but very engaged. As each module and scenario was presented, he willingly voiced his responses. He looked remorseful and his words demonstrated this. The men who come on the course, have normally been arrested a few weeks beforehand, so the events are fresh in their minds. As I asked Ali and the other men on the course that day, “Whom, if anyone, have you told you are here?” Ali said, “I’ve told my wife!”

He explained that on the night he was arrested, it was the first time he had sought to buy sex. For the first few days after the arrest, he was wracked with guilt and remorse. He couldn’t sleep or eat and felt terrible about what he had done. He couldn’t bear the fact that he had broken the trust of his wife and after a few days the guilt was so heavy, he told her what he had done. She was devastated, not only because of the breach of trust, but the cultural shame this brought on their family. She moved out into one of her wider family’s homes for support so this was now something he was going to have to live with in front of others. His wife was still considering if she could forgive and work through this or if the marriage was over; explaining why he looked so broken. You could have heard a pin drop in the room. I was moved by his honesty, which I had not witnessed to that point and told him that I respected his decision to be honest with her. The other men said they would not have the courage to do that. The wider ripples and consequences of the choices Ali made that night, would not only impact the rest of his life, but the rest of his wife’s and family’s as well.

The Impact on Communities

There is a wider impact on communities, particularly from street prostitution and its associated issues, such as the harassment of local women by men looking for prostitutes, littering from discarded condoms and syringes, fear of associated crimes such as drug dealing, robbery and coercion and that children may witness soliciting and sexual activities. Police teams regularly respond to anti-social behaviour (ASB) and issues related to prostitution and I don't want to minimise the impact they have on neighbourhoods. Addressing ASB problems in communities alone, however, merely serves as a sticking-plaster to an open wound.

StreetlightUK's outreach teams are out late at night across London every week. They work hard to minimise ASB and to encourage women to be mindful of residents – to put used condoms in the bin, for example. In one of the areas where we support women on the street, there is a residents' group with one or two vocal members who put a lot of pressure on both the police and local authority to just remove the women. In that same local area, right on the street where the women are, there is an empty doctor's surgery that has been vacant for several years. The police and NGOs, including StreetlightUK, have worked hard but without success, to be able to use this space to support women late at night. Years on, after lengthy consultations with residents and community groups, it still sits empty, when it could be being used to tackle the deep-rooted issues women on the street face. Residents are rightly concerned about the on-street prostitution and its impact but local authority leaders must take a more long-term approach to solving both the ASB and the needs of those most vulnerable on the streets. The police themselves know that just doing a sweep of arrests of women, only pushes the issue into a neighbouring borough. It puts women at significant risk, as they lose contact with support services and is never a long-term solution. Women will migrate back to the areas they know, after several months of laying low. What women and therefore communities need, are safe spaces, right where the issue is happening, so women can quickly and easily access support.

Choices and Consequences

When it comes to "choice," we are careful at StreetlightUK, to ensure that this word is not associated with women, the reasons for which are laid out in a previous chapter. However, the word "choice" I believe very firmly, should be associated with the men involved in buying sex. A man does not just happen to buy sex or buy sex by accident, or as a mistake. He buys sex because of a choice, or a series of choices that led him to hand over money for sex. Men on our perpetrator course will tell us, "It was a mistake" or "I didn't plan to buy sex; it just happened." What they mean is they didn't wake up that morning and plan to go out and buy sex. Having said that, some men do exactly that and plan it into their diaries each week. But most of the men we see are first-time buyers and first-time offenders. This means, they have bought sex many times before but never been arrested and charged. So why is it not a mistake or an accident? Well, for a man to be arrested, with his trousers down, some intention has gone into him getting himself in that position. Men will tell us, "It just happened." We educate men to take responsibility, to see it didn't just happen but was a choice to roll down the window of their car and speak to a woman. It was a choice, to agree on a price and let her get in the car. It was a choice to drive to a secluded car park and get out of the front seat and into the back seat. It was a choice to hand over money. It was a series of decisions, from which a different choice could have been made at any moment.

Every choice we make has consequences. We live in a blame culture where so often, people don't want to take responsibility for their actions, which is why it is always someone else's fault. People say, "It can't be my fault that I tripped up because I wasn't looking where I was going. It must be the council's fault." "It's not my fault that she knocked on my car window at the traffic lights and offered me sex." Sometimes there are reasons why people make bad choices. For some of the men attending our courses, they have just split up with partners, lost jobs or have a sex addiction. But the reasons should not justify the wrong choices. Without taking responsibility for choices and blaming others for their actions, men will continue to make decisions that lead to harmful consequences in purchasing sex. For the men on our courses, the consequences are sometimes life changing. A loss of employment, a loss of reputation in the community and for some, a lost marriage. Charity leaders, university lecturers, teachers, business owners, as well as many skilled and unskilled professionals have all attended our course.

Once a man has a criminal caution on his record, it will also show up on any DBS checks or if he applies for a mortgage. The consequences go on for many years, as many employers require regular DBS checks such as Transport for London (TFL). We get quite a few taxi drivers, lorry drivers and self-employed businessmen who use their vehicles for their work, on our courses. TFL and other employers take a zero-policy approach to their staff being arrested, especially if it involves the vehicle they use for the public in their work. So, although men who come on our course may feel initially that they have got off lightly with just a caution and having to attend a course for a day, in reality, there are ongoing and sometimes devastating consequences to the choice they made that night to buy sex.

Consequences

It is revealing how most men that are referred to us, have never thought about the consequences of their actions when they buy sex. We all impact others through our behaviours and being aware of the consequences of our choices is vital to healthy relationships and healthy lifestyles. Men on our courses seem to find it incredibly hard to express how they feel. Most men we speak with are not used to thinking about why they made the decisions they did on the night they were arrested. A lack of consequential thinking led them to irresponsible action; sometimes with dire consequences. For instance, what happens if a man is the eighth man that night to buy sex from a woman, who is then murdered by the ninth man she sees? His DNA is still all over that woman and his five-minute blow job results in him now becoming a potential murder suspect.

When the police discover who he is, they will not phone and book an appointment that is convenient to speak to him. They will come to his workplace or bang his door down in the middle of the night and arrest him in front of anyone in the house. The fact that he is not guilty of the murder, will not make it any easier for him to live down the consequences of that arrest and the label now associated with him, of being a murder suspect. Many local authorities also have a name and shame policy in place with local media, which will publish in local papers those breaking the law for buying sex on-street. As we tell the men on our course: One wrong choice can have a lifelong consequence. Once the information is out there, it is a consequence they and their families will have to live with – Google never forgets!

Partner of a Former Escort

James, whose partner was a former Escort, contacted us because of the impact of prostitution on both his partner and their relationship. He wanted to volunteer by speaking to the men on our "You Choose" courses.

He said, "I am twenty-five and up until recently, I would have described myself as a typical young man when it comes to sex. I have watched porn regularly since I was young. The way they spoke, behaved and were treated created this fantasy world which never felt real and I never really questioned it. I never considered that the women in the videos were daughters, sisters and mothers and used to be innocent children." He went on to share, "The way women are advertised, from the names to the pictures and bios, conveys this sense that they are sex-obsessed and desperate to pleasure strangers. They are completely dehumanised. If these sex-obsessed fantasy creatures want to accept money to sleep with me, then that's their choice and I don't need to consider or confront the damage it might be causing because they aren't real people like me, my family members or loved ones. I am now in a relationship with someone who spent three months working as an escort. Processing this together has been incredibly painful at times, but has transformed my view of women, men and sex, including my past behaviour and attitude. I have seen first-hand the immense damage and hurt that buying sex causes."

Deterring Sex Buying

Melissa Farley's study on how men describe their feelings after using a woman in prostitution is, "I'm not satisfied in my mind," "looking for more partner satisfaction," "regretful and remorseful," "disappointed – what a waste of money," "angry at myself," "morally at odds," "confused," "lonely – still," "psychologically dirty," "guilt about my relationship with my wife," "asking myself what has led me to this."[38] Similar comments are made regularly by men attending our "You Choose" course, "I had a panic attack," "I was ashamed of myself" and "I feel deceitful and guilty of breaking my partner's trust."

Most men who complete our course show a strong attitude to change and to not buy sex again. I'd like to say they all do this because they want to become part of the solution, in changing attitudes towards women in prostitution. I know for most; their reasons are selfish and not because of the impact on the women involved. With the backdrop of eight out of ten men's first-time experience of prostitution being encouraged, or accompanied by a male friend, or family member, we challenge men to be the "first man standing." What does that mean? It means to be the first man among their peers, their work colleagues and male family members, who say "No!" No to sex tourism, no to stag do's involving prostitution, no to watching porn movies of women – many of whom have been forced into it from childhood. Instead of being part of the problem, which as sex buyers they currently are, to be the first man standing – to be a part of the solution and to say "No!"

> ***A woman can be at a buyer's door within an hour – just like a pizza! That's how easy it has become to access prostitution in the UK.***

Chapter 7
The Money Makers: Whom Prostitution Empowers

The sex industry, or "sex trade" as many abolitionists would like to refer to it, is full of exploitation and financial abuse. At the heart of the issue are those making enormous amounts of profit, often at the expense of those who are most vulnerable. I'd like to share Sophia's story, which shows the complex and mountainous journey that many women face, to become financially independent:

Sophia contacted StreetlightUK after many months of no contact to say she is ready for support. The previous contact was a text check-in once a month for seven months. Sophia was reserved about her experiences but was now comfortable enough to meet with a support worker at her property, where she felt most safe. Sophia moved to the UK ten years ago from Estonia and had been involved in the sex industry since. She had been controlled by a pimp, had all her savings stolen and admitted at times, she thought about ending her life. During the COVID-19 pandemic, Sophia met a man from Estonia and they became friends. He then went on to assault her and left her on the streets of London during the pandemic. She sat in a doorway crying to herself when a member of the public approached asking if everything was OK. Sophia politely advised the woman she was fine and wanted to be left on her own. Sophia began to panic when she noticed the woman had called the emergency services and alerted them to where she was. Sophia said an ambulance, police and two paramedics advised she needed to go with them despite telling them she didn't want to. Sophia was held at the hospital against her will, being told that she was a danger to herself. She was given antipsychotic medication and felt no one was listening to her.

After ten days in the hospital, she finally saw a psychiatrist and was able to explain she was not a danger to herself and the reason she was sitting in a doorway crying was that she had been attacked. The psychiatrist stopped all medication immediately and advised Sophia she was free to leave. Homeless, with no access to funds and no proof of earnings, she was unable to rent herself a property, so she slept on the streets for a while. She finally found a friend who agreed to take out a tenancy in his name for her on the basis she promised to pay the rent each month. Sophia stuck to her promise and still lives in the property paying her rent each month. Her ambition is to become self-employed recycling materials into craft items – something she loves to do. With StreetlightUK's support, she is planning for the future.

Adult Platforms

A few years ago, I was approached by an "AdultWork" business manager to ask if StreetlightUK would like to partner with them to "help" women. I viewed their request with great suspicion, knowing that they are effectively making millions of pounds each year from the individual adverts posted on their site. Before this, I had seen a recent report in the media about women involved in the online adult industry, where "AdultWork" was quoted on their website as "protecting" women; how reassurances had been given by them to the home office of measures taken to support women at risk of exploitation on their site. For those not aware, "AdultWork" is the equivalent of a Facebook platform for the sex industry and the market lead advertising platform for adult services in the UK. According to the Beyond the Gaze report, during three months in 2017, AdultWork reported that twenty-nine thousand eight hundred and twenty-six adult service providers were verified as advertising on their platform. A former escort told me adult sites charged her between five and ten pounds a day to advertise on the site. This is giving AdultWork and other platform providers a potential of over fifty-four million pounds in income annually! These figures don't include the money being made from webcamming and private galleries on adult sites as well. AdultWork does have a support service page on its website on which StreetlightUK and other support agencies are listed. However, our experience of connecting with women on AdultWork and the other adult industry platforms – of which there are many – has not been an easy one.

Whilst many would argue that being able to advertise services and "work" online makes prostitution much safer for those involved, this is often not the case. We meet women at StreetlightUK who are extremely isolated through being involved in online sex. They receive regular abuse and threats which they are less likely to report due to it being online. Women fear being stalked or being found out by neighbours or punters, who threaten them. If women do not feel safe in their homes, where can they?

It is illegal to place a prostitution advert on or in the immediate vicinity of a public telephone (under Section forty-six of the Criminal Justice and Police Act 2001). However, at present it is legal for websites to host those same adverts.[39] As a result of this online regulation gap, highly lucrative "pimping" websites currently operate openly and legally in England, Wales and Scotland. Some overtly advertise schoolgirls or young women. The purpose of these websites is to profit from the advertising of individuals for prostitution. The websites charge fees to the individuals who place adverts, while it's free to use by sex buyers. Sex buyers can simply scroll through and select women who they want to pay to have sex with. They can choose their geographical location, size, hair type, eye colour, type of sex; the list goes on. Sex buyers contact the seller directly via a mobile phone number provided in the advert and a woman can be at a buyer's door within an hour – just like a pizza! That's how easy it has become to access prostitution in the UK.

Men's Reviews of Women Online

After a man has paid for and had a sexual encounter, men can also leave a review on adult platforms, just like when you buy a product on Amazon or other online shopping sites. In their article, 'Myth: Punters respect the women they buy', Nordic Model Now says, "The site owners and users declare that they support, review, patronise and approve only those escorts who are working in prostitution of their own free will. However, when an escort's demeanour shows aversion, even repugnance, punters' only concern is that they are not getting what they paid for." They list dozens and dozens of reviews by men on individual women's profiles such as:

- "She was just distant, uninterested and quite cold, did not perform well and did not care at all about the paying client."
- "Little was on offer in terms of service, enthusiasm, responsiveness or conversation. If she had worked anywhere else, she'd probably have been sacked."
- "I could have been shagging the pillow and gotten more response ... I'm paying for this and expect a decent service ... I can only assume she hates what she does."
- "I'm sick of paying for sex, getting nothing more than robotic treatment and being smirked at on my way out of the place."
- "The main event was like shagging a dead fish (No reaction from her at all)."
- "She was not the least bit interested ... cold and monosyllabic ... as lively as a corpse."
- "It just felt as though she was going through the motions ... needs to learn some dedication to her job."
- "She was completely disinterested and made no effort, an absolutely lacklustre performance ... and she couldn't wait to get out of the room."

- “Cold, clinical, unfriendly and to be avoided. I hope they send her back to Romania.”[40]

These demeaning comments only fuel the ingrained message that women can be used and abused online. An inquiry by the All Party Parliamentary Group (APPG) on Prostitution and the Global Sex Trade, found that two pimping websites dominate the “market” of online prostitution advertising: Vivastreet and AdultWork.[41] The inquiry found that the use of pimping websites is part of the modus operandi of organised crime groups that traffic women into and around the UK for prostitution. In 2017, nine men were convicted for their role in a prostitution ring that trafficked young Romanian women around the Northwest of England and Northern Ireland. The trafficking gang advertised the women they sexually exploited on Vivastreet. In total, eleven women were identified as having been exploited by the group. However, some of the Vivastreet adverts placed by the group included photos of women who were not identified by police.

The Online Safety Act 2023

In its written evidence for The Online Safety Act, the APPG on Commercial Sexual Exploitation summary made two clear recommendations: Firstly, the bill must legally prohibit pornography websites from making their content available to anyone under the age of eighteen and ensure pornography websites are required to adopt robust age verification mechanisms. It is a big milestone and important move forward in protecting our children in law, that this first recommendation has been accepted. Secondly, in their recommendations, the APPG found that the bill failed to make adequate provisions to protect people who may be at risk of commercial sexual exploitation because the draft bill did not prohibit the operation of pimping websites. There is substantial evidence demonstrating that these websites facilitate sex trafficking and sexual exploitation in the UK. To protect individuals vulnerable to commercial sexual exploitation, they stated it is vital that the Online Harms Bill legally prohibits websites from hosting prostitution advertisements.[42] Thankfully, an amendment was made to the draft bill to include adverts that, "cause or incite prostitution for gain and controlling prostitution for gain." The Online Safety Bill has passed all its parliamentary stages and at my point of writing is soon to achieve Royal Assent, meaning it will then become law. At that point, Ofcom will formally act as the regulator for online safety. With hundreds or thousands of adverts on multiple adult platforms online, this is a mammoth task that will need substantial resources to ensure it is effective. However, it is critically important this is carried through in practice.

Ann Marie Morris MP for Newton Abbot states on her website, "The Online Safety Bill is intended to ensure that the internet and wider online environment is a safe place and that tech companies are rightly held to account. Within the Bill, Schedule Seven sets out priority offences, specifically illegal content which amounts to a criminal offence. For example, this includes threats to kill, harassment, stalking, encouraging self-harm and supplying drugs. Also listed as an offence, by the Sexual

Offences Act 2003, is causing or inciting prostitution for gain, and controlling prostitution for gain."[43] Having this included is vital in arming law enforcers to hold to account adult platforms, where there is an epidemic of exploitation of those involved in prostitution.

On 14 July 2023, Diana Johnson MP questioned the Government on how they are tackling the potential exploitation of women on adult platforms. She was particularly asking whether ministers or officials have held discussions with Adult Services Websites on ending the practices of (i) allocating account managers to high-spending customers, (ii) allowing the same phone number to be used in multiple concurrent adverts and (iii) allowing single individuals to post multiple concurrent adverts on behalf of others – all of which leave women open to exploitation. Sarah Dines MP, Parliamentary undersecretary at the Home Office, acknowledged that Ministers have not held discussions with adult services websites. She stated that the purpose of home office officials and law enforcement meetings with adult services websites was only to raise awareness of the risks of online sexual exploitation and the steps companies can take to minimise criminality on their platforms.[44] It seems to me highly ineffective to simply "raise awareness of the risks" of exploitation to the very businesses making vast sums of money from those using their sites. Much more needs to be done to hold the adult platform providers to account.

Women are the Easy Targets for Police

The APPG on Prostitution and the Global Sex Trade pointed out that policing and enforcement of prostitution are unevenly prioritised and resourced throughout the country. They stated that the lack of a centralised political strategy had resulted in disparate local enforcement. End Demand and other campaigners for the introduction of a sex buyer law, believe that enforcement is unfairly targeted at female sex workers rather than male sex buyers. In 2013/14 there were more charges for loitering and soliciting ("selling sex") than for the crimes of pimping, brothel-keeping, kerb-crawling and advertising prostitution combined. Similarly, in 2014/15 there were four hundred and fifty-six prosecutions for loitering and soliciting, yet only two hundred and twenty-seven prosecutions for kerb-crawling.[45] "Sex Worker" Open University agreed that there was clear evidence that sex workers were currently more likely to be penalised than buyers and went on to explain that a variety of measures were used against them, "Most criminal sanctions suffered by 'sex workers' are not reflected in centralised prosecution statistics. They instead take the form of cautions, anti-social behaviour orders (ASBOs), arrests and indeed simple harassment by the police. To take one example, Ilford police station arrested at least one hundred 'sex workers', handed out two hundred and thirty-six cautions and issued six ASBOs in the year to September 2013. It is of particular concern that a so-called 'prostitutes caution', can be issued at police discretion, without the supposed offender even making an admission of guilt."[46] In addition to this, the conviction rates for those brothel-keeping or controlling/inciting prostitution for gain, are disproportionately low – revealing not only sex buyers but also third parties profiting from prostitution, are not adequately being held to account.

Case Study

Mai was referred to StreetlightUK by a partner organisation in Sussex. Initial contact was made when Mai phoned to speak to a member of the team. Originally from Central Asia, Mai married a British man she met whilst selling sex. He brought her back to the UK to live over twenty years ago. They had a child together but they soon divorced and she was left living alone in Kent. Mai wanted to exit prostitution but felt trapped as she did not fully understand the UK system and was struggling to pay rent. She was also supporting her family back home, as she is the oldest of a large family of siblings relying on her. She had indefinite leave to remain but had lost her original passport and only had a copy. To get another one, she was advised she would need to go to Central Asia which she couldn't afford. With long-term support from StreetlightUK, Mai is no longer engaging in prostitution and is happy to be out of the industry. She described escorting as a prison sentence. She now feels like a bird that has been set free. She said, "Prostitution is very easy to get into and very difficult to get out of."

COVID-19 and Prostitution

The COVID-19 pandemic was a horrific time for women in prostitution. But what has that got to do with the money-makers involved in prostitution? As is often the case in any major national crisis, it is the most vulnerable or marginalised in society who are often impacted the most. Every vulnerability our women had was exacerbated by the lockdown, particularly financially. What we witnessed was truly shocking and the shock waves continue today. Before I expound more on the devastating impacts our women experienced, I want to explain the parallel and significant impact our staff and volunteers experienced.

Frontline Staff and Volunteers

As many charities do today, we seek to employ those with lived experience of the issue we are addressing. For one of our staff, the pandemic produced such stress due to this fact. For her, keeping the boundary between her work for our charity and her home life was a key coping mechanism that enabled her to work in this field in supporting women in prostitution. When the pandemic hit and we were all forced to work from home, for her, this meant a breach of that boundary. It brought the issue right into her home; into her safe place. This was just too much and for her mental health and wellbeing, she was unable to work until we returned to our office.

Immediately after the lockdown was announced by the Prime Minister, like every other charity, we lost the majority of our volunteers' availability overnight. Alongside this, the demand for support from our service users increased dramatically. From day one of the lockdown, we quickly moved to remote working, providing IT equipment for staff to enable them to work at home as they no longer had access to office computers. We quickly moved to increase staff working hours to tackle the increased demand and began looking at a new recruitment plan for volunteers. We also saw the opportunity online and used the successive COVID-19 lockdowns to increase our staff/volunteers training sessions. This gave us a much greater uptake from volunteers, particularly in the third lockdown, with new volunteers now eager to join our teams in London and across the southeast. We had to be inventive and work around people's ability and availability to work remotely and those willing to be part of our frontline support on the streets late at night in London. Whilst the majority of the country's workforce was stepped down at home and unable to work, our staff and volunteers' workload increased threefold!

The phones were busy with women who were shocked, isolated and distressed. So, our staff had to be inventive and find new, safe and confidential spaces to work within the home, which was incredibly difficult, as many employees have children. This was significantly noticeable when making calls to women, containing sensitive and confidential content. This was not easy. One employee had to work in her car and another in her bedroom, during telephone calls, as they just didn't have other appropriate rooms in their houses to work. Thankfully, after three weeks of lockdown, StreetlightUK staff and volunteers were deemed key frontline workers and given police permission to be back out on the streets late at night supporting women. This eased a lot of pressure, as they now had the opportunity to see women face to face and the confidentiality of the office space to speak with women during the day.

It was a very humbling eighteen months later, to see these initiatives and the challenging work of our volunteers recognised in 2021. StreetlightUK received the MBE for charities, being awarded The Queens Award for Voluntary Service. Alongside this, we were also recognised as one of only thirty-four charities nationally to be given a second award by the Queen, in recognition of our outstanding frontline response to the COVID-19 pandemic.

COVID-19 Impact on Women

The first three weeks of the lockdown in March 2020 were the hardest and produced tremendous adversity for women who had their only source of income removed overnight. Although our staff faced the initial difficulty of adapting to working remotely, it was our service users who experienced the greatest shock. Women involved in prostitution were affected considerably and exposed to a range of impacts which included financial, mental, emotional and physical harm. We witnessed an upsurge in crisis in about every area of life you can imagine for our women. Homelessness increased across London and the rural counties of Sussex and Surrey, with many women who had previously been sofa surfing with friends, now unable to do so. There was increased substance abuse and suffering from withdrawal symptoms; especially from women not being able to access drugs. Some women were forced to stay in violent relationships due to the pandemic as they were unable to leave home situations where domestic violence and abuse were taking place.

We saw an increased number of sexual attacks on women on the streets, especially in the first lockdown, which resulted in one murder and one stabbing by the same individual, now convicted and in prison. We also saw increased suicide attempts, with one service user attempting suicide within the first four days of lockdown. The immediate loss of income for some women meant extreme financial challenges in lockdown. Due to the hidden nature of prostitution and those involved, many women had no access to the furlough scheme, so couldn't pay rent and feed themselves and their families. This consequently caused intense stress and pressure to an already vulnerable group of women and their families. We also found that some women, particularly eastern European and south American women, became trapped in the UK because of the COVID-19 lockdown. Women on holiday were unable to get a flight home, which subsequently led them to turn to prostitution as a means of survival.

Starving Women

In response to the crisis, due to our amazing staff and some exceptional volunteers, we were thankfully able to double our night-time outreach and support. Daytime support also increased, as more self-referrals and agency referrals poured in. We increased our outreach to women working online, facing higher levels of isolation and began providing homeless women with mobile phones which enabled them to stay connected to support services such as StreetlightUK.

Having been involved in working to support some of the most marginalised women for the past twenty-five years, I've listened to and witnessed women experience some horrific suffering. So, it takes quite a lot to shock me. However, I saw things during the COVID-19 pandemic that shocked me to the core. I write even now with tears, three years later, as I remember women running to us on the streets of north London who were starving. Pre-COVID-19, our teams had not had to feed or clothe women on the streets, but from the outset of the pandemic, we were sharply made aware of its impact. We witnessed women on the streets who were starving, one woman I saw, whose stomach was distended from malnutrition. This was something I had witnessed with starving children in Africa, but never in my wildest imagination thought I would see on the streets of London.

Our response was to immediately start providing food and clothing – 'Sue's sandwiches', were quickly being snapped up and are still the most loved food item by our women today. We provided soft drinks, chocolate, soup and pot noodles. We found funding to introduce an outreach van. This helped us carry and deliver hot food, drinks, coats and hats/gloves throughout the winter months. Initially, I had thought these interventions would only be needed temporarily to get us through the pandemic, but it has become apparent that the ongoing impact on the economy, and the following financial and cost of living crisis has made this a permanent and increasing response.

The Men in Lockdown

I am about to write about what I still find hard to reconcile in how some men treat women. I've described in detail the impact of the pandemic on women involved in prostitution, much of which would have easily been predicted in such a traumatic crisis that the pandemic lockdown produced. What I did not expect was what we experienced from the men during lockdown. For the women, they were forced out onto the streets by extreme financial need and hunger, just to survive; but what about the men? As Sue and I, one of our volunteers, drove with some trepidation to our first night outreach in north London, we wondered what we would encounter. It had been three weeks with no contact with those on the streets. Would they still be there, how would they be, would there be any men present? Our faces were masked with Paddington bear masks. This was in an attempt to try to bring some light conversation to the women; our hands doused in sanitiser and bags full of supplies we arrived at what initially looked like quite deserted streets.

Over the subsequent weeks as we conducted weekly outreach, what became very apparent was that there was no shortage of men willing to break the law and put women on the street at risk, to pay for sex; putting women at risk, their families and themselves, to this unknown virus that was killing millions globally. The men were out in numbers. I understood why women would take such extreme risks due to their desperate situation but I could not understand the men – they were not going to die if they didn't have sex! Yet the streets were often full of men. As we approached the Christmas of 2020, women told us it was particularly busy over the Christmas lockdown holiday season. With a plethora of media stories of politicians from all parties breaking lockdown, perhaps that wasn't surprising. However, for me, it was incalculable that men would take such risks if not concerned for themselves, selfishly unconcerned for their families.

> ***When looking at the core reasons why people buy sex, the ease of accessibility of pornography online must be recognised. Excessive pornographic content has a direct correlation with individuals buying sex.***

Chapter 8
The Online Underworld

A Sexualized Society

It doesn't take expert observational skills, to recognise that modern western culture has become very sexualised. We live in a world where our eyes and ears are assaulted daily by images and sounds that are very sexualised. Turn on the television, browse through the internet, or walk through a shopping centre to witness this. When my children were both in primary school, this was sharply brought to my attention when we were out shopping in the local centre.

We lived in a small market town in Sussex that was prosperous and a lovely place to bring up a family. The high street was pretty and had an array of local independent traders, with a lovely Saturday farmers market to add on top. So, when the new addition of an Ann Summers underwear shop was introduced to the centre of the small shopping centre, it made some waves. I first became aware of this new addition, on a shopping trip with my two small girls for a treat. The new Ann Summers shop was positioned close to the main centre fountain, in the shopping mall which our children loved to visit and play around at. As we neared the fountain, our eyes quickly became aware of the newly installed Ann Summers shop front display. Models dressed in very erotic and skimpy underwear were in full view, along with an array of sex toys in the full glare of my now wide-eyed children. They were asking, "What's that mummy?" and

"Can I have one?" to a large dildo displayed in the window. Looking back now, the situation makes me chuckle but at the time I was angered to have to deal with this unwelcome sexual intrusion on my children's shopping trip.

Over the coming weeks, along with a few friends, I set about challenging the shopping centre management, as I discovered some of the items were being displayed illegally in the shop front window. Ann Summers shops can display sex toys in their shops, but only in designated eighteen and over areas, at the back of their stores. This was being breached and due to our pressure, the items were removed out of view and to the back end of the store. It was a small victory and some might argue an inconsequential one. From that time on, however, it opened my eyes to the other shop front displays at the time. I was struck as I walked through the town, with new eyes, by how many shop fronts had sexualised images of women in their displays. It was everywhere. No more has this been seen than in the online world. Technology transformed access for both adults and children to everything, including sex.

Music: Sexualised Lyrics

In a news report by Sydney Cobb, he stated, "I've always been struck with how the power of music can impact us." With two teenage daughters, I became aware of the challenge of parenting them through a myriad of choices, when it came to what they listened to. This also exposed them to language that potentially would shape their worldview, their view of themselves and their view of sex and relationships. My eldest daughter's passion for music in her teens led her to pursue a degree in music business; after a lot of hard work and dedication, her career took off, and she is now a venue manager at one of the most prestigious music event venues in the UK. Recently, she was awarded UK Female Venue Manager of the Year, (proud mum moment, I just had to slip in). In her dissertation for her degree, she focused on the use of bad language and gender stereotypes in the music industry and how they impact women, particularly in the rap industry. Normalising sexual language through music, has and is, sending strong messages to young people – especially young women – about how they can expect to be treated sexually.

"Through the music industry many want listeners to believe that its lyrics do not affect social norms. Taylor Swift and a host of experts are singing a different tune. A media controversy sparked in February 2023, in response to Kanye West's sexualized lyrics that took credit for Taylor Swift's fame. West defended his song 'Famous' on social media, saying, 'First thing is, I'm an artist and as an artist, I will express how I feel with no censorship.' The 'Famous' feud and its lyrics, now immortalised on West's new album 'The Life of Pablo,' raise questions about misogyny, content and censorship in the music world. It's a conversation that has been going on for years as the lyrics heard in popular genres of music have become measurably more violent and sexual. But does the increase in explicit lyrics influence its listeners?"[47]

In a study titled 'Exposure to Degrading Versus Non degrading Music Lyrics and Sexual Behaviour Among

Youth', Steven C. Martino and his associates tracked a group of adolescents over three years to assess the correlation between the music they listened to and their sexual behaviours. They found that sexually degrading lyrics correlated with higher rates of sexual activity in adolescents. "Our research ... does suggest that degrading sexual lyrics do more than go in one ear and out the other," Martino's study said. "It may be that listening to popular music, regardless of its content, results in heightened physiological arousal that, through a process of excitation transfer, incites sexual behaviour among teens."

Martino said in an interview that degrading lyrics were defined in the study as those that portrayed women as objects and men as sexually voracious and insatiable. They also included lyrics that portrayed sex as inconsequential. "I think that these kinds of messages are prevalent in popular music, and they're not always the kinds of messages that we're looking for as parents. They can be subtle," Martino said. "Degrading sexual content doesn't necessarily mean explicit sexual content." Martino and his team found that among kids with the highest levels of exposure to sexually degrading lyrics, fifty-one percent went on to initiate sexual intercourse between the first and second surveys. For those with the lowest levels, only twenty-nine percent initiated sexual intercourse. "We're talking about kids that are twelve, thirteen and fourteen years old. They're very impressionable," Martino said. "It's a time when they're looking to the media, their friends, and their parents for guidance. We need to look at the messages they're getting before it sets a lifelong pattern of behaviour." Hall, who teaches a class on sexuality education at BYU, fears that adolescents will confuse the lyrics of popular music with social norms.

Prostitution Online

In 2020, The Josephine Butler Society held an afternoon of talks in London, which I attended with interest; expecting the findings would confirm my own experiences with women. Their speakers included Dr Rosie Campbell OBE, from the University of Leicester. Dr Campbell presented findings from research on the safety, working conditions and regulation of sex work entitled, 'Beyond the Gaze.' This project ran from 2015 to 2018 and is the largest study to date of online prostitution (as opposed to street-based prostitution). It provides a qualitative mapping of the sector with its survey of six hundred and forty-one prostitutes and thirteen hundred clients. The project is not about modern-day slavery but rather, mostly women selling sexual services either directly or indirectly via webcamming. Her research confirms that information technology has made changes in the market, evident since 2000. The use of computers, phones and media has facilitated fluidity and mobility across regions and national borders, which of course can have links with problems to do with immigration. She found that women would have between two and nine jobs in prostitution, both visible work and webcam/escorting/filming/BDSM and other "sex work."[48]

Pornography

When looking at the core reasons why people buy sex, the ease of accessibility of pornography online must be recognised. Excessive pornographic content has a direct correlation with individuals buying sex. An increased probability of having paid for sex was identified in men who were dissatisfied with their sex life as well as frequent pornography users. Sex life characteristics such as poor sex life satisfaction, high online sex activity, and frequent pornography use are strongly associated with sex purchases. [xxviii] The perception of women shifts and changes to view females as objects; something which can be bought. They no longer receive the same treatment and respect as other females as they are seen as lower than others. This is where aggression and abuse start to come into play hence why so many female sex workers get verbally abused, beaten, raped and in extreme but not uncommon cases, murdered. A recent and tragic example of this was the murder of one of StreetlightUK's service users in Enfield in 2021. William M. Struthers explains, "Men seem to be wired in such a way that pornography hijacks the proper functioning of their brains and has a long-lasting effect on their thoughts and lives." With the growth of online porn being viewed by an increasing number of young boys, we should rightly be concerned.

Pornography: Impact on Children

With this growth of the sex industry online, a huge concern is its impact on children. With many women involved in prostitution starting before they were eighteen, I have been keenly aware, with two daughters of my own, of its impact. There is no doubt that children are being exposed to online pornography on an alarming scale. Government analysis of statistics from 2015 revealed that in a single month, one point four million children visited pornographic websites from their desktops. Half (seven hundred and thirty-two thousand) of these children were aged between six and fourteen years old. Research by the British Board of Film Classification (BBFC) found that fifty-one percent of children aged eleven to thirteen reported they had seen pornography at some point. Over half (fifty-five percent) of eleven to thirteen-year-olds who have seen online pornography, said they had only ever seen online pornography by accident.[49]

Viewing online pornography can have a deeply harmful impact on children. A survey by the Institute for Public Policy Research found that seventy percent of eighteen-year-olds felt that pornography can have a damaging impact on young people's views of sex and relationships.[50] A poll by the NSPCC's Childline of twelve to thirteen-year-olds found one in five had seen pornographic images that had shocked or upset them.[51] Research by the BBFC found that twenty-nine percent of children who said that most of the pornography they had seen was intentionally viewed, believed that consent was not needed if, "You knew the person fancies you." In comparison, only five percent of children whose interaction with pornography had mostly been by accident believed the same. These stats should concern us. The Department for Culture, Media and Sport has stated, "Existing research indicates that pornography, and its proliferation on the internet, is a concern amongst young people, as well as their parents and carers. Longitudinal studies have also established possible links between the viewing of hard-core or violent pornography by younger people and increased sexually aggressive behaviour later in life." One controlled longitudinal study found that male adolescents' pornography use, predicted their perpetration of sexual harassment two years later."[52]

Grooming: The Signs

A question I often ask when presenting at conferences or events is, "Would you recognise if your daughter, sister, granddaughter or friend was being groomed? Would you know what to look for; what questions to ask?"

Sophie Hayes' story is a stark warning for all parents in the UK. Groomed for years by someone she thought was her friend, Sophie was trafficked from the UK to Italy for sex. For five years, her abductor learnt everything about her and her family in what she thought was a trusted relationship. She had never seen him angry or heard him swear; he was always there for her. So, at a low point when she was just eighteen, he invited her abroad for a weekend break, to take her mind off things. He seized Sophie's passport and made threats to her and her family. He forced her onto the streets in Italy to sell her body for sex. For six months, seven days a week, this was Sophie's life: a life of abuse, sexual exploitation, manipulation, sleep deprivation and starvation. He had trapped and manipulated her. After six months of mental and physical abuse, Sophie stumbled into a hospital, sick and exhausted. Here, she found the courage to call her mother.[53]

Especially for parents and those responsible for caring for children, knowing the signs and what to look out for, is so important. On StreetlightUK's website, we dedicate a page to this, for that reason.[54] This is not a comprehensive list but some of the warning signs are:

- Girls are often identified online and in places like shopping centres, parks, schools and recreation centres. It's critical to understand where children spend their time when they're not at home or in school.
- Boys (sometimes much older) befriend young girls. Then they could introduce her into a gang culture. With the backdrop of two point nine million lone-parent families in the UK in 2022 and a staggering eighty-four percent of them being headed by a lone mother, this is a real draw for young girls, who will naturally look for male role models early in puberty.
- Offer to take the girl out for a drink, offer drugs, shower them with gifts and a new mobile phone. Phones are often given as a form of control, so they can track movements and send messages.
- Flattering girls, pouring on compliments, building a deep emotional bond in young girls, who find it hard to break away from.
- Encouraging them to despise or mistrust parents, family and friends to control them. Girls will often

then become depressed, afraid and display secretive behaviour.

- In the final and worst-case scenarios of grooming, girls who are now brainwashed and “in love” or just under the control of a groomer, are taken to wasteland and “broken in” – beaten up or raped by the gang leader, whilst other members watch and record on mobile phones. Now there is not only shame from the attack but evidence that can be used against them as a threat if the young girl refuses to comply.
- Often at this point, a girl or young woman is forced into prostitution.

This generation, despite being the most connected through advanced technology, has become one of the most isolated relationally. Young people are being impacted by our sexualised society, which bombards them on all fronts. Through technology, media, music, pornography and the culture of modern life, young people’s relationships and health – particularly their mental health – are being negatively affected.

Universities and Prostitution

In answering whether prostitution should be considered as legitimate work as some would argue, we need to follow through with that argument. Education facilities across the country would need to support and even promote this as a genuine career option. Most parents would find this an absurd notion to even consider such a plan for their daughter's or son's future. Yet at some of our university's freshers' fairs, they are doing just that. Before I unpack this concept, let us look at some of the current numbers of students involved in prostitution: Save The Student found that 3% of students have done "sex work" and a further nine percent said they would turn to "sex work" in a financial emergency. Jessica Hyer Griffin suggests the real figures are nine percent of students that have engaged in "sex work" because of the catastrophic effect of the pandemic on people's financial positions.[55]

We met a student called Hannah, who reached out to StreetlightUK for support in 2020. She told us she had an awful childhood and was diagnosed with epilepsy and hyperactivity (now recognised as ADHD), meaning she had lots of time off school which led to poor socialisation. Her stepfather began sexually abusing her from an early age. She feels he singled her out because of her health issues and the fact she was in trouble, quite often because of behaviours relating to hyperactivity. She was always known to everyone as the "naughty girl" or the "mouthy girl." Living with ADHD, epilepsy and regular sexual abuse took its toll on Hannah which resulted in her going into the care system. In her early twenties after being away from the family home she decided that she was not going to let her stepdad get away with the abuse. She spoke to her mother who believed her immediately. A court case was pursued but unfortunately, the predominantly male jury did not believe her. Hannah told us, she will never forget the look of triumph her stepdad gave her when she bumped into him accidentally after the case. This incident completely re-traumatised her.

She then decided that she would turn her life around and achieve an undergraduate degree and then went on to study for a master's degree. It is at this point that Hannah entered prostitution, determined to pay off her fees before completing her Master's. Hannah, now in her late thirties, petite and very self-conscious, reached out to StreetlightUK for support. She said she felt fearful that people around her could simply tell the industry she was in. She had no one else to confide in, leaving her very isolated. We supported Hannah, to look at other ways to fund her postgraduate study. She said if there was another way then she would want to exit prostitution as she hates the work. Hannah realised the long-term effects of staying in the industry far outweighed any short-term hardships she would encounter whilst finishing her master's. Hannah's dream was to finish her studies, build up a good reputation in her new academic field, meet a nice guy, get married and have a family. A week after meeting with our support staff, Hannah decided to exit prostitution with immediate effect. We were able to support her in accessing a grant which was enough to cover her tuition fees, with some money left to live on.

On the Save the Student website, this is what students involved in prostitution say about their experiences:

- "I only did it once and got ten pounds from it. I'd like to do it more, but my boyfriend wasn't too keen on the idea."

- "It's not my favourite source of income ... but I've managed to learn the difference between fake and genuine people online but there are still some crooks out there."
- "I think there is a problem with the system if people have to turn to selling their bodies to support themselves."
- "Strange men sometimes message me on Facebook and ask me for the weirdest things, and I will do it if it doesn't include me being nude."
- "I had sex for money, it lasted two minutes and I made one hundred pounds."

Alice told the Daily Record she signed up with an agency which said their clients liked students and at the start, things seemed good. Alice was sexually assaulted by one of the clients and then told by other female sex workers they had all experienced it and she was lucky. She said, "The other girls said I'd been lucky, it was only a matter of time, it happens to us all and we get over it."

Universities that have published guidance relating to student sex workers have come under fire, with critics accusing them of legitimising and encouraging the trade. Brighton University was criticised for allowing a sex workers health and support service to run a stall at a freshers' fair. The University of Leicester issued a guide called, 'Student Sex Work Toolkit for Staff in Higher Education.' It details how to support those who turn to escorting, online services and stripping. Staff are advised not to be judgmental or assume the student wants to leave the sex industry. They should also, “challenge university policy which allows ‘sex workers’ to be expelled for ‘bringing the university into disrepute,’” it says.[56]

> ***Having witnessed a monumental change with the smoking ban in 2007, I am confident and convinced that the same shift can happen in the public's perception towards prostitution in the UK – if we are bold enough to try!***

Chapter 9
What's Next? Solutions

Dreams Really Can Come True

I would like in this final chapter to focus on solutions. I have always been a positive thinker who sees the positive aspect in everything. There are genuine routes out of prostitution for those who wish to stop, who can then go on to live whole, full and fulfilling lives. Why do I believe this? Because I see it every year with the women I work with. There are women who are incredibly resilient and brave and have a gut determination to change their lives for the better. They have a determination that enables them to not just put behind them the extraordinary challenges, abuse and trauma, but to reach out and achieve their dreams and ambitions of a brighter future, for themselves and their families.

This is not an exhaustive list, of what I believe needs to be in place to effectively protect and support women, who wish to exit prostitution. However, it represents twenty-five years of seeing women's struggles and some of the challenges they face in this field. There is some amazing work already being done, in a growing number of prostitution specialist services across the country, like StreetlightUK. Their staff and volunteers are made up of some of the most incredibly compassionate and self-sacrificing women you will ever meet. However, we need many more specialist organisations if we are to see real and lasting change in supporting women and disrupting the growing sex trade in the UK.

Exit Support Programmes

I would like to begin by looking at how we help women exit. Nine out of ten women we support at StreetlightUK tell us, “Please help me to get out.” Women involved in prostitution often fall through the current nets in statutory services. This is why specialist charities like StreetlightUK are so overwhelmed with meeting the needs presented to us. This is demonstrated in the vast array of referrals that we receive from the statutory services. From Police, Sexual and Mental Health teams, Doctors, Probation services and Education bodies – to name just a few of the routes into our service. Yet, over seventy percent of our referrals are still self-referrals from women themselves, often as a direct result of our outreach to them. Many local authorities have a Violence Against Women and Girls (VAWG) forum and some have a sub-group dedicated to prostitution, such as the Lambeth Sexual Exploitation and Harm Panel, (SEHP). Prostitution is happening everywhere, in every village, town and city across the UK. We need fully resourced exit support programmes, built into every local authority. This should include a dedicated VAWG specialist staff member or team of specialists, depending on the prevalence of prostitution within the area. With the backdrop of evidence presented in ‘No Little Girl’s Dream’ and in the vast array of research materials, articles and other books available, it is at best naïve and at worst negligent for legislators to think otherwise and to fail to fully resource accordingly.

Gathering the Data

From the inception of StreetlightUK, I quickly became aware that there was extraordinarily little documented, up-to-date data, or evidence of the scale and nature of prostitution in the UK. I quickly came to realise that it would be down to grassroots organisations, like StreetlightUK, to put in the leg work, to discover the real facts about who is involved in prostitution and its impact locally. Local authorities, police and other statutory-funded bodies are simply not resourced to capture this information. Even though jointly they have a statutory and, I would argue, a moral duty to do so, their very existence is to serve the communities they represent – particularly the most vulnerable and marginalised. When establishing StreetlightUK, I knew it would be vital to gather the evidence to demonstrate the need I knew existed. I also knew with absolute clarity that what was needed was a specialist support service, for women involved in prostitution. We didn't need another project attached to an existing service for domestic violence or homelessness for example. Rather, we needed a specialist, expert service entirely focused on the issue of prostitution. Whilst I know several projects nationally, that do an excellent job in tackling this issue, as part of a wider organisation for domestic abuse or homelessness, I have also seen the downside of such organisations, adding on a sex work project. With competing priorities for resources within organisations, staff are often spread too thinly and women in prostitution lack the dedicated support they deserve.

This group of women seemed to me to be falling through the nets of every other service. So, with a clear mission, I initially spent two years researching prostitution across Sussex. Visiting the local homeless and substance abuse projects, I spoke with police, local authorities, churches and community groups, who had their finger on the pulse of the issue (and crucially, speaking with the experts – the women themselves!). As StreetlightUK has developed its service over the past twelve years, this has become an embedded practice, of conducting monthly detailed research into the scale and nature of prostitution across London and the Southeast. We meticulously detail and document the prevalence and impact of prostitution on those we support. We create opportunities throughout our organisation and working practices that allow the women we support to strategically inform and shape our service. Working with specialist partners and statutory bodies must embed this same level of analytical research in an ongoing way into their community services. Strategies that are only updated once every three to four years and that only scratch the surface of the issue, are simply not enough. Systems to obtain accurate and up-to-date information on the scale and nature of the issue in every local authority, need to be put in place.

Specialist Services – Why They are Needed

Over seventy percent of women who self-refer to StreetlightUK are not engaging with any other services. They are often not registered with a local doctor or able to access some of the most basic agencies they need. Many are only made known to the local authorities when a tragedy such as domestic violence, rape or an overdose takes place and they end up in the local accident and emergency department. This was best evidenced to me when we met Joan, who lived in a rural town in Surrey and was in her seventies.

We initially contacted Joan through our online outreach service and after initial contact was made, Joan phoned to speak to a member of the team. She was living alone and so happy to have someone to speak to. Joan described herself as a typical escort with a "bad father in childhood." She got into debt because of escorting because she was living a luxurious lifestyle and said it was so easy to spend the cash because she, "paid for things to make herself feel good after doing this horrible job." She was very self-aware as to how earlier experiences of trauma such as rape and abortion impacted her decision to sell sex. Due to the COVID-19 pandemic, Joan moved to engage in phone sex chat and had increased her phone sex as it provided her with some company. She said she doesn't particularly like doing phone sex as it is, "bad for the soul." Joan also had some physical health issues which she had been paying for through private healthcare, so she was tempted to return to prostitution to pay for this, but we explored other ways to produce an alternative income. To relieve some of the financial pressure, we supported Joan in getting some of her debt written off, due to her age and living situation. During her time in the sex industry, Joan had worked independently for agents and in brothels. She admitted that mostly, she continued to sell sex due to loneliness, as she found her persona in her alter-ego. She wasn't close to many members of her family, many of whom lived abroad and didn't know of her involvement in prostitution. Joan quickly communicated to us that she wanted to exit prostitution and wanted to use her experiences to benefit and protect other women in the industry. She helped us create a safety leaflet, which we now use to support other women. Joan told us that in the twenty-two years of being in the sex industry, no one had ever reached out to help her before.

Twelve years on from my initial research of prostitution, this group of women still don't quite fit anywhere in the statutory world. The NHS, police, sexual health, mental health and substance abuse services are regularly engaging with this group of marginalised women, but without specific training or an in-depth understanding of how best to engage with and support them. Since StreetlightUK's inception in 2012, we have had regular referrals from a wide range of professionals, who frequently tell us they feel ill-equipped to offer the support they can see women involved in prostitution need. We regularly hear women tell us, "You are one of the very few people in my life that I can openly talk to about my actual real life ... not a lot of people know what I do and the ugly side of life."[57] "When StreetlightUK first reached out to me, I ignored them and then they reached out to me again and again and I thought, 'Wow, there are real people who care about me!'"[58]

Provision of support for those involved in the sex industry has often been described as a "postcode lottery." The 2017 Mapping the Maze report mapped services for women facing multiple disadvantages. In England and Wales, only nineteen areas out of one hundred and seventy-three had services for women that addressed all the following issues: substance misuse, mental health, homelessness, offending and complex needs. The report also identified only twenty-four specialist projects in

England and Wales providing support for women in prostitution. Whilst this mapping did not capture all specialist projects operating across England and Wales, there are still vast areas of the UK lacking access to specialist support.[59]

A Consistent Police Approach Nationally

In 2018 in London, I attended a 'Beyond the Gaze' report feedback meeting, which presented the findings from research on the safety, working conditions and regulation of sex work. During the presentation, a Police Constable who works to support anyone subjected to sexual violence, and under-reported crime across London said, "The situation is not helped by the fact that there are thirty-two boroughs in London with diverse approaches even though they all aspire to target devious perpetrators. Only about 10% of victims do contact the police."

A consistent approach across police teams nationally is urgently needed, that is victim-focused and not enforcement-led.

StreetlightUK has developed an effective model of partnership working with police teams over the last decade. This has not been easy, with layers of policy and constant movement in established police teams. Relationships with local ward officers are vital, as they know and care about their "patch." However, if they are only in place for eighteen months or short periods, then local knowledge and intelligence are often lost. More problematic is when effective solutions are being delivered together at a grassroots level on the ground by police teams and local partners, which suddenly get cut. A decision from above cuts or diverts the team to other priorities, often without consultation and with devastating consequences. We have seen the impact of this, repeatedly – particularly with the Metropolitan Police in London. Consultation often only happens once the decision has been handed down from above, leaving local police and partners left to try and find a way forward. The stark reality for the women we support on the streets of London is that they suffer. They can lose vital access to support services, as police teams enforce or “sweep clean” the streets. They are driven to unfamiliar places and the problem is pushed onto neighbouring boroughs. At worst women die, losing the tiny threads of support that have kept them from falling over the cliff edge of hopelessness and isolation. Having worked with hundreds of police teams at all levels over the past decade, I know there are some exceptional men and women, who care about the issue, many at a local ward level. However, their hands are often tied and decisions must be translated into a coordinated and consistent approach in practice. If something is working, why try and fix it? This expresses how often partners are left feeling. National Police Chiefs Guidelines are just that – guidelines. But these are not enough if not followed through in practice.

Target The Demand: Sex Buyers

Women and men continue to receive different punishments for their involvement in the same crime: soliciting for sex.

This becomes clear in the police approach of arresting and prosecuting the easy targets: the women on-street. There is no doubt that policing and enforcement of prostitution is unevenly prioritised and resourced throughout the country and that the lack of a centralised political strategy has resulted in disparate local enforcement. Within London alone, one borough may be diverting women into exiting services whilst another is focused on clean ups and crackdowns. Policing of prostitution is inconsistent because enforcement of legislation is resource intensive.[60] It rarely becomes a policing priority unless an extremely serious case is reported.[61]

To combat this, police forces nationally must ensure that they adhere to the National Police Chiefs' guidance for 'Sex Work.'[62] However, what is the point of having guidance if it is not implemented on the ground? All police forces must appoint a full-time Police 'Sex Worker' Liaison Officer (SWLO) as set out in the guidance – liaising to build trust and encourage reporting with women and agencies supporting women. Rather than arresting women, this should focus on investigating and monitoring the crimes against 'sex workers' and ensuring training across police forces is consistent and their policies and systems are developed to respond to hate crimes against those involved in prostitution.

Safe Spaces for Women

The guidance also sets out what is called a pillar of 'Creating safer spaces.' Where police forces are to ensure there are women-only safe spaces, that are within easy access – particularly for those involved in prostitution as survival sex who are homeless or on-street. My experience of this in London, as expressed earlier, is that empty council-owned properties can sit empty and unused for years – right in the heart of the "red light" districts, despite multiple attempts by specialist outreach services to bring them back into use. Councils battle between balancing the needs and challenges residents face at having prostitution and drugs on their doorsteps and providing support to the women on-street. Often a few vocal voices of residents win over the dozens of vulnerable women, who often have no voice other than through support agencies. Having a safe space, late at night on the street, where women can report crimes and receive support is vital. An important addition is to have facilities such as a place to receive hot food, a shower, and sexual health swabs in the cases of those who have been raped or sexually assaulted. There are often small windows of opportunity in supporting women with chronic needs and simply asking them to come to the police station the next day is not effective.

Tackling Online Crimes

Police Teams need to be fully funded to tackle online abuse. Currently, the police teams we work with in Sussex, Surrey and across the Southeast rural counties are under-resourced to tackle the mountainous abuses taking place online. With hundreds of thousands of prostitution services being advertised on dozens of adult platforms (some fake, and some exploitative), there is a huge task for police to do in tackling this. We regularly feed through reports to the police from our online research, where we come across suspicious adverts, or ads promoting schoolgirls or other obvious crimes. We initially started working with Sussex police teams in 2012. I have to say that they are an exemplary police force in their determination to tackle sexual violence. They have a clear focus on supporting victims of crime and arresting those involved in exploitation and crimes against women (particularly crimes such as stalking, domestic violence, rape and sexual exploitation). Sussex, Gatwick and Surrey Police forces, often in a combined manner, run regular operations to tackle prostitution, which StreetlightUK staff accompany them on. However, even with such a proactive approach, police teams are still not effectively able to meet the demand due to limited resources. Government money needs to be redirected specifically to support local police teams in tackling online crimes against women in prostitution. With increased students and young people turning to prostitution, due to the cost-of-living crisis, this is urgently needed.

UK Policy: A Mixed Approach

Some countries, including the UK, do not have one clear position adopted in law and instead have a mixed policy approach. This means certain activities linked to the sale of sex are criminalised, such as soliciting and certain activities relating to the purchase of sex, such as kerb-crawling. The actual approach taken towards the sale of sex may depend on the local government and whether they take a hands-off approach, police the violence towards people involved in prostitution, or control prostitution as a public nuisance. A mixed approach like this often makes the policy environment confusing and sometimes hostile to those most vulnerable in the sex industry. It is also exploited by those third parties, such as pimps, gangs and online platform providers, who are profiting from the sex industry. Police teams across county and borough boundaries need clear and consistent policy and legislation. This can empower them to tackle criminals and the crimes being committed.

Legalisation Does Not Work

I'd like to first summarise the arguments made by those advocating for the full legalisation of prostitution. Advocates of full legislation argue that we will be able to see and control the abuse better because it won't be underground. It shouldn't be hard for people to engage in prostitution because it could turn punters violent. Such people argue that the sex industry shouldn't be reduced because women should be able to make an income from it. Therefore, they advocate that we should normalise prostitution so that those selling sex are not stigmatised. However, as evidence shows from the numerous models of fully legalised sex industries in the Netherlands, Germany and New Zealand, when demand grows so does the black market with associated exploitation and harms. Further, even in the "visible" and "legitimate" establishments, it is easy to hide exploitation and women do not report abuse for fear of repercussions.[63]

More than ninety percent of the males attending our perpetrator course inform us that making it more difficult for people to purchase sex will discourage them from doing so. Making it harder – not easier – reduces the risk of harm by removing more potential perpetrators. Violence still occurs in legalised/decriminalised systems and punters who are driven by violence are not put off either way. In countries where it is a criminal offence to buy sex, there are fewer instances of women involved in prostitution, who are murdered. The stigma around prostitution is such that even in legalised systems, women do not want to register themselves. Focusing on legislation that enables women to participate in communities in tangible ways should be an overriding goal.

The Society for the Advancement of Socio Economics (SASE) is an international, interdisciplinary organisation with members in over fifty countries on five continents. In their report, 'Two Failed Experiments' they stated, "The impact of commercialisation is the most important aspect of prostitution and is largely ignored in policy debates. It is its commercialisation that leads to enormous amounts of exploitation and modern slavery, because people are using human beings to profit and/or capitalise on their economic needs to coerce them into sex and a variety of sex acts. The reality of a prostitution transaction is that consent is being bought and 'bought' consent is not free and enthusiastic consent borne out of mutual attraction."

Another argument made about full decriminalisation and legalisation is that it is not possible to reduce demand at the same time as helping women to be safer. StreetlightUK's model of partnership with police teams across the southeast debunks this argument. Having successfully seen over two hundred and forty men arrested and attending our courses, we have reached a ninety-five percent success rate in deterring re-offense (alongside our frontline teams supporting thousands of women not only to be safer but for many, to find routes out of prostitution).

It has been shown that even without changing the law, it is possible for policing prostitution to avoid criminalising people selling sex and instead offer support, while also challenging men's demand for sex (Matthews and Easton 2011; Poland 2008). This is achievable even without changing the law and has been a successful approach in both Ipswich and Glasgow. Buyers and pimps should not have free licence, in order for those selling sex to receive the support they need.

A Sex Buyers' Law

Criminalising the purchase of sex, often referred to as 'The Nordic Model' has so far been adopted successfully in Sweden, Norway, Iceland, Lithuania, France, Finland, Canada, Israel and Ireland. The Nordic Model has three key factors, each of which is essential for it to be effective in law and in protecting women. These are: decriminalising the sale of sex, criminalising those who purchase sex or profit from the pimping of women selling sex and offering service provision to exit prostitution.

Currently, the burden of the law sits on the women, in that they are the easy target to arrest and criminalise. A sex buyer law in England and Wales that criminalises the pimping and purchase of sex, shifts that burden onto the buyers. It moves it off women and onto men who make up most of those profiting and purchasing. This criminalises the demand.

Thirteen years ago, the government of Sweden published an evaluation of the law's first ten years and how it has worked in practice. Its findings were amazingly positive: street prostitution cut in half; no evidence that the reduction in street prostitution has led to an increase in prostitution elsewhere, whether indoors or on the internet; increased services for women to exit prostitution; fewer men state that they purchase sexual services and the ban has had a significant effect on traffickers who find Sweden an unattractive market to sell women and children for sex. Sweden appears to be the only country in Europe where prostitution and sex trafficking have not increased.[64] Critics want to challenge the Swedish facts but they speak volumes and should be listened to and acted upon in the UK.

An Abolition Agenda

Harm minimisation is not enough to keep women safe. It is not politically correct to talk about abolition or an eradication agenda but in my view, they must be not only talked about but given the political airtime needed in debate. Only then will we truly offer long-term solutions to the trauma and harm that prostitution is causing women. Current legislation is very much focused on harm minimisation, but the 'Nordic' model offers an opportunity for women to change their lives and leave prostitution. We can never truly keep women safe by simply offering condoms, but only by providing specialist support for them to exit. It's important to see that this dovetails into the agenda to reduce trafficking – modern-day slavery, as we see a growing number of women being controlled by organised gangs. Some but not all local authorities operate a name-and-shame policy, fines and deterring reoffending courses, which all help reduce demand. The harder we make it for those who purchase sex to do so, the more we disrupt and deter the demand. This approach would effectively empower the police to protect those most vulnerable to abuse in the sex industry. Evidence in Sweden and other countries that have adopted the Nordic Model demonstrates that lives are significantly improved as a result.

In an environment where there is a big focus on lived experience, the voices of those who have exited prostitution should be listened to. The current public narrative often dismisses the voices of the very people who have first-hand experience of the trauma and abuse experienced in the sex trade. Women who have exited have told us at StreetlightUK that they wished they had met us and had access to exit support sooner. Their welfare should be foremost in all policy decisions.

In Sweden, where the police have the power to intervene and investigate prostitution, there has been only one murder of a woman involved in prostitute since the law changed. This murder had nothing to do with her involvement in prostitution and was instead to do with her ex-partner and custody of her children. In contrast, in the

Netherlands over the last thirty years at least one hundred and twenty-seven women involved in prostitution have been killed[65] and in Germany, since 2002 at least thirty-four have been killed, as well as twenty attempted murders. Violence continues to be a huge problem in legalised countries. The International charity CARE has stated, "Given the harm experienced by women involved in prostitution, it is entirely legitimate to seek to reduce instances of the sale of sexual services." Likewise, considering the harm caused to those selling sexual services, it is entirely appropriate that the weight of the criminal law should focus on those who create the demand or who profit from it. Although there are many factors which might cause an individual to enter prostitution, without buyers, there would be no prostitution. The most effective way to reduce the harm of prostitution and trafficking for sexual exploitation is to reduce the demand for paid sex.[66]

A National Campaign

I have spoken about this in detail in chapter six but I believe a vital solution needed in every local authority where prostitution is prevalent, is fully funded deterring re-offending programmes. This must be a triune partnership between the police, the local authority and specialist support services, to effectively challenge and educate those purchasing sex. The programmes should operate in conjunction with an enhanced UK Nordic Model law that criminalises sex buyers and is built into sentencing conditions, with an emphasis on educating men and disrupting the current acceptability of paying for sex among certain groups of men. At the heart of this program should be a focus on changing public perceptions around prostitution, just as has been achieved in Sweden. As demonstrated in Sweden and other countries, changing the public perceptions of prostitution is certainly achievable in the UK. With focused leadership by lawmakers working in partnership with support services to highlight the harms, this undoubtedly, can be achieved.

To effectively implement this, a campaign under the 'Minister for Women and Equalities for the Equality Hub' should be set up to coordinate and implement a national advertising campaign. This campaign should target exposing the harms of prostitution, just as the smoking ban campaign did in 2006/7. Through local governments, it should be broad reaching to have a national impact, reaching into Education, Local Government policies and Media outlets across all platforms. The smoking ban in the UK was successful because of a long and national campaign, beginning with studies in the 1950s, demonstrating the link between smoking and lung cancer. They demonstrated the harm and did this on a national scale with radical results. The same approach should be taken with prostitution. It is not a normal day-to-day "job" for women and we should call out its normalisation. Having witnessed a monumental change with the smoking ban in 2007, I am confident and convinced that the same shift can happen in the public's perception towards prostitution in the UK – if we are bold enough to try!

> ***Without a doubt, the legal focus in the UK needs to shift off the women involved and onto the role of sex buyers and pimps who perpetuate the industry.***

Conclusion

I recently heard Dr Krish Kandiah OBE speak to a couple of hundred exclusive community, civic and statutory leaders across East Sussex. Krish is a theologian, author and activist, and works with the government to improve the lives of vulnerable children in the care system. He told a story of taking forty pounds out of a cash machine, which was delivered to him in two twenty-pound notes. One was crisp, new, and looked like it had come straight from the Bank of England Royal Mint. The other, he said, "looked like it had come out of my pocket after a weekend at Glastonbury ... it was scrunched up, dirty and stained." He went on to ask the audience the question – which had more value? He highlighted, of course, that their value was the same. How some people are presented in society, including women involved in prostitution, has meant they have not been viewed with the same value, dignity and respect as others. We have accepted the normalisation of their dehumanisation, when in fact, their worth is intrinsically the same as those considered the greatest among us.

I've highlighted how prostitution is a complex issue that cannot be understood solely in terms of criminal justice or public health perspectives. The nature of prostitution varies widely across different regions and populations and there is no single "typical" profile of the women involved. It is often linked to other forms of exploitation and abuse, including human trafficking, drug addiction and homelessness. It is clear prostitution takes a significant physical toll on women, from sexually transmitted infections to physical violence. The health risks associated with prostitution and the lack of access to healthcare for women in the industry are indisputably harmful. Likewise, the emotional trauma women experience include depression, anxiety, and post-traumatic stress disorder with long-lasting and devastating impacts (not least of which is women's mental health). The psychological impact of prostitution is affecting many women's relationships and their ability to trust others.

Without a doubt, the legal focus in the UK needs to shift off the women involved and onto the role of sex buyers and pimps who perpetuate the industry. The motivations behind those buying sex and how it contributes to the exploitation of women should be seriously addressed by legislators and law enforcers.

We need to work towards ending prostitution. We must identify this harmful practice as a form of violence against women. This will go a long way in order to create a more just, and equitable society for women, including increased access to education, job training, and mental health support. Legislators have a pivotal role in bringing systemic change and increasing awareness around the harms of prostitution nationally. The facts paint a compelling argument for why prostitution is *no* little girl's dream!

About the Author

With over 30 years of frontline involvement, Helena is an experienced visionary leader and public speaker. She is a former Council Deputy Leader and expert in understanding sexual violence and the exploitation of women. Helena is the Founder and Chief Executive of the award-winning Charity StreetlightUK which has successfully supported many thousands of women involved in prostitution over the last decade.

With a strong focus on finding solutions, Helena has cultivated an in-depth knowledge of the most pressing issues facing women in the modern world. She has worked amongst some of the most marginalised and vulnerable individuals in society, establishing several successful community projects throughout London and the Southeast. As an activist and role model for women from all walks of life, Helena is committed to shining a light on the lives of some of the most hidden among us; telling their stories and ensuring their voices are heard.

Helena was awarded an MBE in the King's Birthday Honours List 2023 in recognition of her outstanding contribution to the charity sector, particularly in supporting vulnerable women and those impacted by modern slavery.

About StreetlightUK

StreetlightUK is a frontline specialist service for women involved in prostitution and all forms of sexual violence and exploitation – including those trafficked into prostitution. Founded by Helena Croft MBE, the charity provides tangible pathways for women to exit prostitution. StreetlightUK has developed its specialism and understanding of women across London and the Southeast since 2012.

In 2022–23 StreetlightUK directly engaged with over six thousand six hundred women, supporting over six hundred women involved in prostitution across London and the southeast. An expert service in tackling violence against women and girls, StreetlightUK enables women to overcome the multiple challenges that limit their choices: lack of education and employment opportunities, as well as the physical and emotional barriers they face. The service also focuses on the root causes of why women are involved in prostitution, such as poverty, low self-worth, sexual abuse/violence, mental illness, addictions and lack of support relationally.

In partnership with the Metropolitan Police, StreetlightUK also delivers a deterrent re-offending course for men arrested for soliciting on-street sex; educating them on the consequences and impact of their choices on women and the wider community. Over two hundred and forty men have completed the course since 2018 with a ninety-five percent success rate and in one borough a hundred percent success rate, in deterring re-offending.

In June 2021, the charity received the Queen's Award for Voluntary Service, the MBE for charities. They also received an extra award given to only thirty-four charities nationally from the Queen, in recognition of their frontline support during the Coronavirus pandemic.

www.streetlight.uk.com

About PublishU

PublishU is transforming the world of publishing.

PublishU has developed a new and unique approach to publishing books, offering a three-step guided journey to becoming a globally published author!

We enable hundreds of people a year to write their book within 100-days, publish their book in 100-days and launch their book over 100-days to impact tens of thousands of people worldwide.

The journey is transformative, one author said,
"I never thought I would be able to write a book, let alone in 100 days... now I'm asking myself what else have I told myself that can't be done that actually can?'"

To find out more visit
www.PublishU.com

Bibliography

[1] Speech at the Massey College Fifth Walter Gordon Forum, Toronto, Ontario, in a symposium on 'The Future of Feminism.'

[2] The S&D Group, n.d. Sexual exploitation and prostitution and its impact on gender equality [Online].

[3] United Nations, 2020. Global Report on Trafficking in Persons 2020, New York: United Nations.

4 APPG on Prostitution and the Global Sex Trade, Shifting the Burden, March 2014.

5 CEASE summit 9 October 2019, Coming together to end sexual exploitation.

6 StreetlightUK Case Study Medway September 2023 WSW KN.

7 The NSPCC's National Policing 'Sex Work' Guidance June 2023.

8 'Sex Work' and Occupational Homicide: Analysis of a U.K. Murder Database.

9 CARE (PRO0078); and APPG on Prostitution and the Global Sex Trade, Shifting the Burden, March 2014, p5.

10 (Cho, et al., 2013; United Nations, n.d.).

11 Church, S. Henderson, M. Barnard, M. & Hart, G. Violence by clients towards female 'prostitutes' in different work settings: questionnaire survey. BMJ,322(7285), 2001 pp 524-525.

12 UNAIDS, 2022. Global HIV & AIDS statistics — Fact sheet [Online].

13 (Home Office 2004a).

14 (Ramsey et al 1993).

15 (Granth Lone et al 2014).

16 [The prevalence of, and factors associated with, paying for sex among men resident in Britain: Findings from the Third National Survey of Sexual Attitudes and Lifestyles (Natsal-3). [Online]. First doi 10.1136/sextrans-2014-051683.]

17 Nefarious – 'Merchant of Souls Documentary' by Exodus Cry (Released in 2011.).

18 Award-winning Charity StreetlightUK, www.StreetlightUK.uk.com

19 Home Affairs Select Committee, Third Report of Session 2016 –17.

20 In sections 51A, 52, 53 and 53A of Sexual Offences Act (2003).

21 Subsection (2) and section 53A, Sexual Offences Act 2003, 2003.

22 Dr. Kate Lister ('sex work' historian). (Lerner, 1986; Amsterdam Red Light District, n.d.).

23 House of Commons. 2019. 'Universal Credit and Survival Sex.' House of Commons Work and Pensions Committee. [Online]. https://publications.parliament.uk/pa/cm201919/cmselect/cmworpen/83/83.pdf

24 House Crown Prosecutors. 2022. 'Public Order Offences Incorporating the Charging Standard.' [Online]. https://www.cps.gov.uk/legal-guidance/public-order-offences-incorporating-charging-standard

25 Pfeffer, R. 2018. 'Women and Men Receive Different Punishments for their Involvement in the Same Crime: Prostitution.' The London School of Economics and Political Science. [Online]. https://blogs.lse.ac.uk/usappblog/2018/03/27/women-and-men-receive-different-punishments-for-their-involvement-in-the-same-crime-prostitution

26 National Network to End Domestic Violence. 2016. 'Can a Person in Prostitution be Raped?' WomensLaw.org. [Online]. https://www.womenslaw.org/about-abuse/forms-abuse/sexual-abuse-and-exploitation/forced-prostitution/connection-between

27 Mire, F. 'How Sex Workers Who are Sexually Assaulted are Being Failed by the Justice System.' inews. 21 August 2019. [Online]. https://inews.co.uk/opinion/how-sex-workers-who-are-sexually-assaulted-are-being-failed-by-the-justice-system-328027

28 Charlotte Deogan et al 2021.

29 The Pimping of Prostitution – Julie Bindel Preface ix.

30 British Heart Foundation. 'What is a Heart Attack?' Uploaded on 19 March 2019. [Online]. https://www.bhf.org.uk/informationsupport/conditions/heart-attack

31 British Heart Foundation. 'Air Pollution.' March 2022. [Online]. https://www.bhf.org.uk/informationsupport/risk-factors/air-pollution

32 (Home Office 2006).

33 (Home Office 2004).

34 Commonwealth Housing (PRO0035).

35 Neuroscience News.com. 2016. 'Men Who Buy Sex Have Much in Common With Sexually Coercive Men.' [Online]. https://neurosciencenews.com/sexual-coercive-psychology-5841/

36 National Survey of Sexual Attitudes and Lifestyles.

37 (Birch & Braun-Harvey, 2019; Monto & Milrod, 2014; Weitzer, 2007).

38 Farley, M. 2009. 'Men Who Buy Sex: Who They Buy and What They Know. Eaves: Putting Women First. [Online]. https://documentation.lastradainternational.org/lsidocs/Mensex.pdf

39 Written evidence to The Online Safety Bill the All-Party Parliamentary Group on Commercial Sexual Exploitation (osb0037).

40 Nordic Model Now! 2016. 'Myth: Punters Respect the Women They Buy.' Myths About Prostitution. [Online]. https://nordicmodelnow.org/myths-about-prostitution/myth-punters-care-about-the-women-they-buy/

41 Vivastreet is owned or controlled by the offshore holding company W3 Ltd, based in Jersey. 'AdultWork' is owned by CDLB Holdings Inc, a company registered in Panama. It is operated by a company called AWS Affiliate World Systems International Limited, which is registered in Malta and also based in Cyprus.

42 Written evidence to The Online Safety Bill the All-Party Parliamentary Group on Commercial Sexual Exploitation (osb0037).

43 Conservatives. 'Online Safety Bill – Sex Workers.' [Online]. https://www.annemariemorris.co.uk/online-safety-bill-sex-workers

44 Parallel Parliament. 2023. Home Office Vivastreet. [Online]. https://www.parallelparliament.co.uk/question/194152/home-office-vivastreet

45 Home Affairs Select Committee, Third Report of Session 2016-17, End Demand (PRO0070).

46 Home Affairs Select Committee, Third Report of Session 2016-17, 'Sex Worker' Open University submission (PRO0147).

47 Sydney Cobb. For the Deseret News. 22 April 2016.

48 Beyond the Gaze. https://www.beyond-the-gaze.com/

49 'Young people, Pornography & Age-verification.' January 2020. British Board of Film Classification.

50 'Child Safety Online: Age Verification for Pornography.' Department for Culture, Media and Sport. February 2016.

51 'Girl, 13, Reveals How Online Porn Turned her Boyfriend into a Sexual Predator, as Study Finds One in Ten Children Fear They are Addicted to Watching Internet Sex.' Daily Mail. 31 March 2015. [Online]. Accessed at: https://www.dailymail.co.uk/femail/article-3019288/Girl-13-reveals-online-porn-turned-boyfriend-sexualpredator-NSPCC-campaign.html; NSPCC Cymru/Wales: A year in review 2014 – 2015. [Online]. Accessed at: 6 https://www.nspcc.org.uk/globalassets/documents/annual-reports/cymru-wales-in-review-2014-2015.pdf

52 'Child Safety Online: Age Verification for Pornography.' Department for Culture, Media and Sport. February 2016, p.39-40.

53 Sophie Heyes Foundation. https://www.sophiehayesfoundation.org/

54 StreetlightUK. 'Signs of Grooming.' [Online]. https://www.StreetlightUK.uk.com/signs-of-grooming

55 Venn, L. 2022. 'Thousands of Students are Sex Workers – Universities Need to do More to Protect Them.' The Tab. [Online]. https://thetab.com/uk/2021/09/20/thousands-of-students-are-sex-workers-universities-need-to-do-more-to-protect-them-222364#:~:text=A%20survey%20by%20Save%20The,work%20in%20a%20financial%20emergency

56 English Collective of Prostitutes. 2021. 'The Mirror: Desperate Students Sell Sex to Pay Fees as Lockdown Kills Off Jobs in Pubs and Shops.' [Online]. https://prostitutescollective.net/the-mirror-desperate-students-sell-sex-to-pay-fees-as-lockdown-kills-off-jobs-in-pubs-and-shops/

57 StreetlightUK Case Study, Lambeth VG.

58 StreetlightUK Case Study, Lambeth SS.

59 Dr Thorlby, K. & Collis, G. 2022. 'The UK Sex Industry: Learning from Frontline Services.' Beyond the Streets. [Online]. https://beyondthestreets.org.uk/wp-content/uploads/2022/01/Support-needs-of-those-involved-in-the-UK-sex-industry-FINAL-for-publication.pdf

60 Home Affairs Select Committee, Third Report of Session 2016-17, APPG on Prostitution and the Global Sex Trade (PRO0158).

61 APPG on Prostitution and the Global Sex Trade (PRO0158).

62 NPCC 'Sex Work' National Police Guidance June 2023.

63 SASE – Two Failed Experiments 2019.

64 Raymond, J.G. (2010.) Trafficking, prostitution and the sex industry: The Nordic legal model. Coalition Against Trafficking in Women.

65 DutchNews. 'Cold Case Team Identifies Possible Prostitutes Serial Killer.' 22 May 2013. [Online]. http://www.dutchnews.nl/news/archives/2013/05/cold_case_team_identities_poss.php

66 CARE All Party Parliamentary Group on Prostitution and the Global Sex Trade which concluded in its 2014 Shifting the Burden report.